LETTERS TO THE SEVEN CHURCHES

by
JOSEPH A. SEISS

Author of "Lectures on the Gospels," "Lectures on the Epistles," "Voices from Babylon," "Lectures on the Apocalypse," etc., etc.

WIPF & STOCK · Eugene, Oregon

Wipf and Stock Publishers
199 W 8th Ave, Suite 3
Eugene, OR 97401

Letters to the Seven Churches
By Seiss, Joseph Augustus
ISBN 13: 978-1-62032-035-8
Publication date 1/13/2012
Previously published by Baker, 1856

This is a reprint of the 1956 Baker reprint
of the printing made in 1889
under the title, 'Letters of Jesus'

PREFACE.

THE Lectures here following were prepared for the author's week-day appointments during Lent. Direct practical impression, and not critical elaboration, was the controlling aim in their composition. As they were preached in different years, some repetitions of thought occur in them which might have been eliminated to the advantage of their literary finish; but as the same things recur in the text, and differ in the form in which they reappear in the Lectures, it has been concluded to leave all as originally delivered.

Lent is by general consent a season arranged by the Church for the calling of its members to a special sobering of their minds for serious meditation upon their situation with regard to spiritual things. It is a time to call to mind the presence and inspection of God, His displeasure with sin, and how we are to secure salvation from it.

It is a time for earnest seeking unto the Lord to discover and amend what is defective in our hearts and lives, and for the quickening of our endeavors to be in full accord with the divine requirements. Christians need such seasons. The sensibility of conscience is liable to become dulled. Our realization of the need of the Saviour, and our hold of faith upon Him as our only hope, require frequent deepening and intensifying. We must betimes turn aside from our ordinary ways and indulgences to consider what we are, where we are, and whither we are going. We cannot make progress in the divine life without oft stimulation to the reverence and ardor of our supplications, faith, and resolves. And, though other times and seasons may and should be used for these ends, Lent, with its special services and prayers, is intended to subserve such spiritual purposes, and well answers to them.

And when it comes to such an arraignment of ourselves before the bar of God to make sure of our estate before Him, it would seem to be greatly helpful for us seriously to take up and devoutly consider these Letters of Jesus to His professing people on the earth. Here we are brought into immediate communication with our living Lord Himself, present throughout His churches, observing everything, and giving His infallible estimates and decisions on what He beholds, commending what is pleasing to Him and condemning what He disapproves and hates. Here we have His own directions and commands according to the situation in each separate case, wherein also He tells us exactly what shall be the result of dutiful fidelity on the one hand and disregard of His Word on the other. And hardly another section of Holy Scripture is to be found better calculated to impress the heart, awaken spiritual consciousness, animate our hopes, and further us in the way of Christian improvement. Hence the choice of it for these Lenten Lectures.

In treating of these sacred Letters the endeavor has been to deal faithfully with the divine Word without regard to anything else, to avoid all rashness and doubtful speculation, and to venture nothing on mere guess or conjecture. It would be presumption for the author to claim that he has in every instance succeeded in accurately voicing and applying the Saviour's meaning;

but in so far as he has light he is quite convinced of the truths he has sought to bring into view. Nor would he have preached these Lectures, or now consent to give them to the public, if he were not persuaded that such as sincerely desire to learn the mind of the Spirit may get from them some wholesome impressions to help them in Christian life, and some perhaps not before so distinctly reached. Certainly, things of very solemn moment to all are here brought into contemplation, and things which should not fail to quicken spiritual life, strengthen holy purposes, dispose to patience under trials, and inflame with zealous desire to obtain the promises which our Lord holds out to the overcomers in the conflict for the immortal prize.

Accordingly, these Lectures are submitted with the hope and prayer that this attempt to draw out and apply "what the Spirit saith unto the churches" may be of service to souls, and redound to the praise of Him who walks amid the golden candlesticks and holds the stars in His right hand.

Table of Contents.

Lecture First.

	PAGE
Christ's Letters to the Churches	17
Common Neglect of these Letters	18
Letter to the Church at Ephesus	19
The Stars in Christ's Right Hand	19
The Golden Candlesticks	20
Christ Amid the Candlesticks	21
His Presence with His People	21
His Close Observance of All	23
The Church at Ephesus	25
Christ's Account of this Church	26
Its Good Works and Patience	27
How it Dealt with False Teachers	28
The Fervency of its Love	29
The Earnestness of its Piety	30
Well-doing Deserves Acknowledgment	31
These People not Perfect	33
No Perfect Church on Earth	33
The Wane of Love	34

Lecture Second.

The Defect in these Ephesian Christians	37
Not in a State of Apostasy	38
Declension in First Love	40
Commonness of this Defect	40
An Easy Thing to grow Sluggish	41
The Remedy Prescribed	42
The Better Past to be Remembered	43
Enthusiasm of First Discipleship	45

	PAGE
Repentance Required	47
Not all Repentance the Same	48
First Works to be Repeated	49
Baptismal Vows to be Returned to	50
Encouragements to Amendment	51
A Serious Threat	52

Lecture Third.

Devout Attention Demanded	54
Neglect of the Divine Word Rebuked	55
Outward and Inward Hearing	57
Christ's Words those of the Spirit	59
The Character and Attitude of True Believers	59
Christians are Soldiers	60
Enemies to be Overcome—Ignorance	60
Carnal Nature	61
Subtleties and Assaults of Satan	63
Promise to the Overcomer	64
Eating and the Tree of Life	65
The Promises Graded	67
Individuality of the Promise	68
The Earthly Church not Saved as a Body	69

Lecture Fourth.

Church at Smyrna	71
The Saviour's Sympathy	72
Tenderly Considers our Weakness	73
Has Respect to our Tribulations	75
Why He Sends Affliction	76
Takes to Heart what His People Suffer	78
Adversities of the Smyrniotes	79
Polycarp and his Martyrdom	80
Trials not to be Feared	81
The Great Matter is Confidence in Jesus	82
Poverty that is Riches	83

Lecture Fifth.

The Church at Pergamos	85

TABLE OF CONTENTS.

	PAGE
The Sword of the Word	86
Moral Surgery	87
Christ's Knowledge of the Situation	88
Unfavorable Surroundings	89
Christ's Name	91
Holding Fast Christ's Name	93
Dutifulness to the Faith	94
The Gospel Nothing to be Ashamed of	95
The Faithful Antipas	97
No Excuse for Unfaithfulness	98

Lecture Sixth.

The City of Pergamos	100
"Satan's Throne"	101
Tenderness of Christ's Censures	102
The Responsibility of Ministers	103
Balaamism	104
Balaamism in the Church	106
Christians Serving the World	109
Great Ailment of Modern Christians	110
The Nicolaitans	111
Not yet Extinct	112
God requires Honest Consistency	113

Lecture Seventh.

Religious Controversy	114
Christ's Judgment on Erring Churches	116
Individuality not lost in Community	117
The Conflict to be Maintained	118
Particular Evils to be Combated	119
Promise to the Victor	120
Manna	121
The Hidden Manna	122
The Glorified Christ	123
The White Stone	125
The New Name	126
Encouragements to Fidelity	127
Voices from Heaven	127

Lecture Eighth.

	PAGE
Thyatira and Lydia	129
Christ's Description of Himself	130
The Son of God	130
Meaning of this Claim	131
Eyes of Flame	132
Many not what they Seem	134
Church at Thyatira not Totally Apostate	137
Some Good Christians there	138
Their Faith and Patience	139
The Hindrances in their Way	140
Church not to be Forsaken because of Evils in it	141
Growth in Grace	142
No Standstill in Christian Life	143

Lecture Ninth.

Best of Churches have Unworthy Members	145
A Plague-spot in the Church at Thyatira	146
Woman in Christianity	147
The Mischief she can Do	148
A Second Jezebel	148
True and False Inspirations	149
"The Depths of Satan"	152
Warnings before Judgment	153
A Limit to God's Forbearance	154
Judgment upon Jezebel and her Children	155
The Burdened Faithful	156
Encouragement to the Tried	157
Deliverance will Come	158

Lecture Tenth.

The Letter to Thyatira for the Whole Church	160
Duties of Christians in this World	161
To Hold and Use the Word and Ordinances	162
To Maintain the Conflict with Evil	163
To Keep Christ's Works	164
Incentives to Faithfulness	166

TABLE OF CONTENTS.

	PAGE
Salvation is thus made Sure	167
Brings to Heavenly Office and Administration	168
Shepherdizing of the Nations	171
Possessing the Morning Star	172
Our Labors here not in Vain	174

Lecture Eleventh.

Sardis	176
The Church in Sardis	177
Christ's Presentation of Himself to	178
Has the Seven Spirits of God	178
The Paraclete	179
The Seven Stars	179
Condition of the Church in Sardis	182
A Name to Live while Dead	183
Christ's Demand upon Them	184
Drowsy Eyes must be Opened	184
What is Perishing must be Strengthened	185
Past Experiences must be Recalled	186
The Reasons Why	187
Probation and Judgment	188
The Crisis Impending	188
Prominence and Power of this Doctrine	189
We Know not the Time	190

Lecture Twelfth.

God has Saints in the Worst of Times	192
Our Judgments Often at Fault	193
The Saints have Garments Undefiled	194
In the World, but not of It	196
Despised on Earth, but Esteemed in Heaven	198
Shall be Clothed in White Raiment	199
The Book of Life	201
Names therein	202
Christ's Confession of His Own	203
Names on Earth and Names in Heaven	204
Great Things for our Consideration	205

Lecture Thirteenth.

	PAGE
The Church in Philadelphia	207
Those who Say they are Jews, but are not	208
False Professors	210
Profession Necessary, but not Sufficient	210
Evil in the Several Churches	211
The Holy One and the True	214
An Open Door	215
Keeping the Word of Christ's Patience	216
Strength in Weakness	218
Safety from the Great Tribulation	219
Translation and Crowning of the Waiting Saints	220

Lecture Fourteenth.

Future Blessedness and Glory of the Saints	224
Who are Saints	226
The Eternal Temple	227
Pillars in it	228
God's Name upon Them	230
God's Priests	231
The New Jerusalem	232
Heavenly Citizenship	235
Inscription of Christ's New Name	236
Our Riches in Christ	237
The Great Possibilities in Life Eternal	238

Lecture Fifteenth.

The Seven Churches Prophetic of Seven Periods	241
Our Times the Laodicean Period	243
Christ "The Amen"	244
The Fulfilment and Authentication of All Prophecy	245
"The Faithful and True Witness"	247
The Only Revelator of God	248
"The Beginning of the Creation of God"	249
The Operating Cause in Creation	249
How Christ would have us Regard Him	250
A Great Thing to Know Christ Aright	251

TABLE OF CONTENTS.

Lecture Sixteenth.

	PAGE
Archippus and his Charge	253
A State of Coldness	254
Not Approved of God	255
A State of Warmth	256
Examples of	257
A State of Lukewarmness	258
Ways in which it is Induced	259
A Lukewarm Christian not a Saved Man	263
Self-satisfied and Self-secure	264
Christians of our Day	265

Lecture Seventeenth.

Liability to be Deceived	268
Self-delusion of the Laodiceans	269
How they became Self-deceived	271
Christ's "Counsel" to them	273
To Buy of Him	274
Gold, the True Riches	275
White Raiment	276
Healing Medicaments	276
Buying of Jesus	277
A Blessed Opportunity	280

Lecture Eighteenth.

Jesus the Chastener of His People	282
All History Attests this	283
Worth of the Discipline of Suffering	283
Prosperity no Evidence of the Divine Favor	285
Chastening a Sign of the Saviour's Love	286
The Rod applied to Spur our Zeal	287
False and True Zeal	288
Zeal Required	290
Repentance the Great Need	291
No Lack of Zeal in the Worldly-minded	294
Christianity Demands it Above All	295

Lecture Nineteenth.

	PAGE
An Affecting Picture of Christ	297
The True Location of the Scene	298
Jesus Unrecognized by His Church	300
Is Loth to Abandon His Church	302
His Standing and Knocking	302
This Knocking here Something Peculiar	303
Some Loud Enunciation of His Presence	305
Marked Agitations in Nature	306
His Last Appeal has a Degree of Violence in it	307
Symptoms of the Nearing Judgment	308

Lecture Twentieth.

Christ's Promises to them that Open to Him	312
Gradation in the Promises	314
Thrones and Dominion	315
Christ's Enthronement with the Father	316
His Own Throne Distinguished	317
The Regency of the Saints with Christ	318
Destiny of the Saints	320
The Greater the Glory the Greater the Conflict	321
The Foes to be Vanquished	321
No Reason for Despair	323
Our Duty to Bid for the Highest Honors	325

Lecture Twenty=first.

Grieving the Holy Ghost	328
God hath Spoken	329
His Word for All People	330
A Résumé of the Contents of these Letters	332
These Things Meant to be of Practical Account	335
Differences in Hearing	336
All is Personal	337
Individual Responsibility	338
Have we Profited by these Letters	339
Conclusion	341

ALMIGHTY and Everlasting God, Who hatest nothing that Thou hast made, and dost forgive the sins of all those who are penitent; Create and make in us new and contrite hearts, that we, worthily lamenting our sins and acknowledging our wretchedness, may obtain of Thee, the God of all mercy, perfect remission and forgiveness; through Jesus Christ our Lord, Who liveth and reigneth with Thee and the Holy Ghost, ever one God, world without end. Amen.

THUS speaks the Spirit to the churches all,
　　And to each man who hath an ear to hear:
　　Whoso o'ercometh in this fell career
With powers of earth and hell, which proudly call
My people to the battle, he shall fall
　　Unvanquished, and to his grave shall bear
　　The martyr's crown; victorious rise and wear
The palm of jubilee.　Let no fears appall
Christ's fellow-soldiers.　Him, your Captain, view
　　Upon the throne of God; Who hath on high
Mansions prepared, and wine o' th' kingdom new
　　Upon His table set; where never sigh
Is heard, or sorrow enters.　There shall you
　　With Him abide, and in His bosom lie.

THE LETTERS OF JESUS.

Lecture First.

Rev. 2 : 1-4: "Unto the angel of the church of Ephesus write; These things saith he that holdeth the seven stars in his right hand, who walketh in the midst of the seven golden candlesticks; I know thy works, and thy labor, and thy patience, and how thou canst not bear them which are evil: and thou hast tried them which say they are apostles, and are not, and hast found them liars: and hast borne, and hast patience, and for my name's sake hast labored, and hast not fainted. Nevertheless I have somewhat against thee, because thou hast left thy first love."

THIS is from the first in a series of seven Letters sent by the blessed Saviour by the hand of the apostle John to the seven churches of Asia Minor. These Letters constitute a unique section of sacred literature. Like the Parables, they consist exclusively of Christ's own words; but, unlike the Parables, they were dictated from heaven after He was risen and glorified. They are perhaps the only unabridged records of His addresses that we possess. They are also so impressively introduced, and so particularly addressed to the churches, as to imply that there is something in them of unusual solemnity and importance. They come to us with a seven-times-repeated admonition to hear them, and lay them to heart. As we have ears to hear, we are commanded to hear what the Spirit saith to the churches.

It is therefore a little strange that there is not another part of Holy Scripture, of equal prominence, to which the Church has paid less attention. The Parables of Christ are continually being brought before us: the discussions of them are endless. But it is rarely that God's people are called to consider these *Letters of Jesus*, though bearing His own sign-manual, and so particularly urged upon the attention of every one. Is this right? Should we not be as anxious to know what Jesus has dictated from heaven, and has commanded us to read, hear, and keep before us, as to know what He said in His discourses while on the earth? Is not the subject-matter in these Epistles as important, practical, and full of instruction as any other part of the New Testament? Why, then, has there been such a common neglect of what our Lord has pronounced so blessed for us to hear, ponder, and digest?

On entering, then, upon a very solemn portion of the Church Year, and meaning by some special services to bring ourselves into closer fellowship with our blessed Saviour, may it not be well for us to occupy these appointments by reverently considering what He has thus sent to His churches, and trying to gather up at least some of the precious things which He has thus given for our learning? And in doing so let us earnestly pray God to open our hearts, that we may duly understand and profit by His holy truth.

In the passage now before us we have the first part of the Letter to the Church of Ephesus, from which we note—

I. *The description which the Saviour gives of Himself:* "These things saith He that holdeth the seven stars in His right hand, who walketh in the midst of the seven golden candlesticks."

This refers back to the vision described in the preceding chapter, where it is clearly explained that "the seven stars are the angels or ministers of the seven churches, and the seven candlesticks are the seven churches."

Ministers are *stars*. They are so designated because they are God's light-bearers, intended to shine on the earth in the Sun's absence. They have their high station for the sole purpose of dispensing light. They are not all of the same magnitude, "for one star differeth from another star in glory;" but the office of every one is to give forth heavenly illumination.

The business of a star is to shine, to give out

light; and that of a minister is the same. A preacher or bishop who does not preach, or whose sermons enlighten no one, may be a minister of man's manufacture, but surely not a star made of God. Stars are of no conceivable use to us except as they give light. They may be very big bodies, have very large circuits, fill an immense amount of space, and be as heavy and ponderous as the sun itself, but if they give no light and have no power to illuminate, they might as well not be, so far as respects us. They only fill up room which might be better occupied. And it is well for us all to bear in mind that as stars are made to shine, so all ministers must be light-bearers and light-givers.

These stars are *in Christ's right hand*. He upholds them. They are His agents and instruments to carry and impart the heavenly light of life and salvation to benighted man. He calls, directs, and sends them. They have their high and beneficent office from Him. And they depend on Him for their place and for the light they give.

The candlesticks are the churches, because it is the office of the churches to hold up that which gives out the light. People may have candlesticks for mere ornaments, displays of rich material and handiwork, specimens of beautiful forms and elegant chasing; but that is not the true use of candlesticks. Candlesticks are meant to hold candles, to support lights. The truest and best candlestick is that which best supports a candle. What we want in it is a secure holder —one that will stand steady and remain firm—one that will receive and support a candle, that we may see by its light. We do not judge it so much by its pattern, its material, or the labor that has been bestowed upon it as by the completeness with which it answers its purpose. When a letter reaches us in the night-time, and we are anxious to know its contents, what care we whether the candlestick is gold or brass or clay, only so that it holds the light by which to see to read? And so it does not so much matter as to the material and organization of a church. The best is that which best sustains the truth and best gives out the saving light.

Now, the description which Christ here gives of Himself is, that He *walks in the midst of these candlesticks:* "These things saith He who walketh in the midst of the seven golden candlesticks."

When on earth He said, "Wherever two or three are gathered together in my name, there am I in the midst of them." From this we see that it does not take a great building, a grand cathedral, or a large assembly of people to make a church. It may be well to have good accommodations and strong congregations; but, no matter how humble the place or small the assembly, two or three united in faith and joining together for the confession and service of Jesus are church enough to attract the Saviour's presence; and there He is "in the midst of them" as much and as really as in the grandest assembly. His disciples may be interested in "the great stones of the temple," but the Master's attention is on something more noble and more enduring. His eyes are on the "living stones" and how they are disposed. While men are admiring the architectural splendors, He is noticing the poor widow with her mite and the soul-sick publican smiting his breast and saying, "God be merciful to me a sinner!" Piles of stones or rocks stationed as if bursted upward into granite blossoms are not the things which most attract our blessed Saviour. Far more is He interested in the gathering of the people in His name, even though it be in some cold barn or lowly hovel. Wherever His people come together for holy worship, there He is. By His word and promises and Spirit and grace He is with them, to hear their prayers and to dispense His mercies. And thus He walks amid all the golden candlesticks the world over, present wherever His name is called and His Gospel sounded.

And, being present with His churches, He observes and notes all that is going on in them and all that pertains to His people. "*I know thy works*" is what He here says of Himself. Nothing escapes Him. Every individual is held in full survey. He sees the private walk, the deeds of worship, the heart of devotion. He beholds the Pharisee in his pride, the publican in his humility; the rich casting into the treasury of their abundance, and the poor offering of their narrow means. He would have the church of Ephesus understand that He knew it thoroughly—all its works, its labor of love, its hatred of evil, its sufferings, its patience, its strength, and its weakness. He has "eyes like a flame of fire," which penetrate all hearts and all lives, which look into the inmost recesses of the soul, and to which all things are naked and open. He knoweth the proud afar off. He looks through all masks and all disguises. No one can cloak or dissemble so as to impose on Him or deceive Him. There is not a thought in the heart, but, lo! He knoweth it altogether. He knows who we are and what we are, and what we have been doing, and with what sort of mind and temper we are now in His presence. "His eyes behold the works, His eyelids try the thoughts of the children of men."

Nor is there a heart upon which the eye of Jesus is not fully set the same as if it were the only heart in the world. If any one's thoughts are wandering, preoccupied with other than sacred things, dwelling on all but what has brought us together, or calculating about this or that, unenlisted in the things that are being said of the blessed Jesus, busy, but not with the spirit of worship and honest desire to come nearer to God, He is observing it and knows it better than that soul itself. Whoever else is absent, Christ is here, for He walks in the midst of the candlesticks, and there is never a moment's suspension of that all-penetrating omniscience with which He is contemplating every one of us here or elsewhere. No matter what is uppermost in our thoughts, feelings, or wishes, what we have been or what we now are, Jesus knows it all. If we have come hither to-day with true heart and a right spirit, He beholds it, and His favor and blessing go out to the soul that is seeking Him and is desirous to honor Him. If prayer and sorrow for sin and penitential longing for His mercy and grace be in our hearts, He observes it and encourages and fans it with His promises and Spirit. If the tear has silently gathered in the eye or fallen in regret over follies past; if the heart has quickened its beating over the pain felt for the wrongs and uncharities by which the life has been marred and stained; if the soul is swollen in the bosom and heaving out sighs to be freed from the condemnation we have deserved,—there is nothing quicker in an angel's wing or in the lightning's flash than the speed with which this is telephoned to the ear and understanding of the divine Saviour. To every one His word is "*I know thy works;*" and neither we nor angels can tell Him anything about ourselves which He does not see and know. Our sorrows which we may not tell, our trials which no other knoweth, our difficulties, our hardships, the woes and aches that lie buried in our souls, our weaknesses and heart-struggles, our hidden fears and doubts, our honesty in things for which others blame and censure, our real motives and endeavors which others do not understand,—all are known to the loving Saviour, who can be touched with the feeling of our infirmity, and bids us be of good comfort, that His grace shall be sufficient for us. There is no child of His unnoticed or on whom His loving eye does not rest, to look subduingly upon the Peters that deny Him, to speak consolingly to the Marys that weep over their sins, to note the secret devotions of the Nathaniels under the fig tree, to commend the faith of the bowed and crippled ones who struggle amid the jostling crowd that they may but touch the hem of His garment.

Note,

II. *What Jesus saw in these church-people of Ephesus.*

We learn from the Acts of the Apostles how they had been gathered and formed into a Christian congregation—how Paul, passing through the upper coast of the Mediterranean, came to Ephesus, and found there some twelve Christian believers, refugees from the murderous persecutions which the malignant Jews were waging against those of this faith in Palestine. God overrules the wrath of men to His own praise. Many churches had their first beginning through the fugitives who were thus driven away from their own country on account of their faith in Christ. Those whom Paul found at Ephesus became the nucleus for the great and honored congregation at that place. They were the first materials in the formation of that candlestick for the upholding of the light of the Gospel amid the heathen darkness of Diana's worshippers. And with the apostle Paul as their minister and champion, whose hands and ministrations they did everything to uphold, great progress for the truth was made. Turned out of the synagogue of the Jews, to which he first went and preached Jesus and the resurrection, they procured the use of a schoolhouse of one Tyrannus, where Paul went daily preaching and arguing with all comers, and convincing and persuading many by his arguments, his testimony, and his miracles. And thus the church of Ephesus was established.

It is claimed by some that Timothy was its first bishop, but there certainly were a number of other overseers or bishops with him, whom the Holy Ghost had made overseers of that church.

It was a highly favored church. Having had Paul for its founder, the venerable apostle John spent his last years in close association with it. It had great privileges, and it had greatly profited by them. It is always well when people gladly hear the truth and live up to it.

The church at Ephesus was a devoted and active church. He who walks amid the golden candlesticks saw their "*works.*" True Christian faith and devotion always bring forth good works. Idle and do-nothing Christians are of but little worth to themselves or to the world, and their Christianity is of a very doubtful sort. It is not said what these "works and labors" were, but we can easily infer them from accounts elsewhere.

The people were in earnest in their religion, and did everything in their power to make converts to it. They upheld and helped Paul in all his efforts to the full extent of their ability. They filled their places with heart and energy, and were zealous for the cause. They worked together for the same end. They exemplified what they professed and believed. They were *Ephesians* in the real sense of that word—full of ardor, warm and fervent in their zeal and activity for the Gospel and the bringing of men to embrace and share the blessedness of it. All this is necessarily implied in what is written, that "the word of God mightily grew and prevailed." And this the Saviour knew, remarked on, and commended.

They also had much "*patience.*" Twice does the Saviour refer to their patience. They were not dispirited, put out, and made to hold back because things did not go just to their mind. They were slandered by the Jews and persecuted by the heathen, but they held on to their faith and did not falter in their endeavors. Trade unions rose up to drive them out of the city, but they stood firm for the Gospel. They had to bear all sorts of taunts, calumny, and ill-treatment on account of their faith and zeal, but they did not retaliate nor give over on that account. They were *patient*—patient in bearing contumely, patient in waiting God's time and will in all things, patient in holding on and working on, oppressive and hard as the situation was. They knew for Whom they were working, and the great interest to the community and the souls of men the establishing a strong Christian church in Ephesus would be, and they were not to be diverted from their fixed and steady purpose, glad to do and suffer in such a cause. And for this Jesus praised and commended them.

Great efforts were made to corrupt them against the truth. Wicked men got among them, but they cast them out. When they could not be moved by opposition and persecution, hypocritical pretensions and deceit were brought into requisition. Men came insinuating ill things against Paul as not an apostle, but an impostor, and others came claiming to be the true apostles and the only true teachers of religion. Deceivers sought to ingratiate themselves with them, that they might pervert their minds and turn them from the truth. But they did not take everything for granted that people said. They were careful to know where things came from and who those were who came with these tales and novelties. They tried them which said they were apostles and were not, and found them liars, and would have nothing to do with them. These blandfaced whisperers, who know so much and are always retailing insinuations of what they have heard to the discredit of good people, found no favor with these Ephesian Christians. And for this also the Saviour eulogized and commended them.

These Ephesian Christians were further characterized by great fervency of love. This was especially the case in their early history. "Adversity makes strange bedfellows," and companionship in common calamities and hard misfortunes tends to unite souls very closely that otherwise would never be brought together. The first members of this church were all persecuted exiles, driven away from their homes and country because of their faith, and as fellow-sufferers in the same holy cause they were very close in their intimacy and warm in their mutual sympathy and regard, which became one of the particular features of the original church of Ephesus.

But their love and interest in one another were only the reflection of a still more ardent love to Jesus and His truth. Had it not been so they never would have abandoned home, friends, and possessions in their own land to take the place of fugitives and refugees in a strange and corrupt heathen city. Their religion was not fashion. They were Christians, not from custom or because it was a reputable thing with those whose good opinion they prized. They were Christians from honest conviction, from genuine principle, and were ready to forsake father and mother, houses and lands, and to become strangers and pilgrims on the earth, out of pure love and devotion to that blessed Saviour who left heaven and died on the cross for them, and had sealed them by His Holy Spirit of promise unto eternal redemption. Nor does anything so enlist, please, and gratify our glorious Lord as to behold such devotion in His followers and children. "I love them that love me" is His saying of old, and His heart ever softens toward those whose hearts are warm and zealous toward Him. It is indeed a beautiful thing to love Jesus, and a very uncomely and wicked thing not to be moved with affectionate gratitude to Him who has so loved us and done so much for us. And as these Ephesians loved ardently, Jesus noted it and commended them for it.

Well-doing and worth deserve acknowledgment and commendation, and the withholding of these when due is not according to Christ. Even though all good in His people is from His grace, and none of it could be without Him and the helping power of the Holy Ghost, when they thus improve under His merciful dealings He gives them credit for it, and expresses His pleasure and approval. Bad men often flatter and praise as a lure to those whom they wish to win to their favor or influence to their own selfish ends. They know the power of praise, and they dishonestly use it. This is despicable. Good people are apt to err on the other side, and are strangely chary and neglectful in the use of this power. Whether it be to gain the respect and affection of others, the moulding of their desires, the guiding of their will, the cure of their faults, or the strengthening of their activities in what is good, almost every other means is preferred to that of commendation. Argument, advice, admonition, warning, and especially rebuke, censure, and complaint, are liberally used; but words of approval and esteem are carefully withheld or grudgingly doled forth, as if some hidden danger lurked in them. The example of Christ was different. Even in this world of sin and sinners He still found some things to commend and praise; and in here speaking from heaven it is the same.

Dishonest praise is wickedness. It is base in him who gives it and evil to him to whom it is given. But candid, truthful, and liberal acknowledgment and commendation of what is right and good is a blessed inspiration both in the giver and the receiver. It draws them together. It freshens and stimulates effort. It begets mutual confidence and multiplies strength. It opens a community of feeling and interest which makes correction of faults easy, serves to correct despondency and faintness, and tends to encourage, cheer, and reinforce. To assure others of your good opinion if they can trust your sincerity and truthfulness animates them to increased effort to justify your favorable regard, and it helps to build up love, good-will, and virtue. It is right, and it is useful. It helps to allay the envious and bad in human nature and to bring out and foster the good. It is a happiness in itself, and it gives happiness. What a comfort and inspiration was it to these Ephesians, whatever there was in them to be corrected, to be thus commended by the Saviour for so many things! How much more courageously would they now exert themselves to repair what was defective, that they might stand thus approved in all things! And if we could but know what failing energies may be refreshed, what languor chased away, what hope and enthusiasm inspired, and what love and confidence begotten by our words of honest, cordial praise, we would not be so backward in our expressions of them.

But, as in all cases in this world, these people were not perfect. With all their virtues, they had their faults and failings, which honest love could not omit to mention and disapprove, that effort might be made to supply what was wanting. With all the Saviour's commendations of them, He still found it necessary to say to them, "*Nevertheless, I have somewhat against thee.*"

There is no such thing on earth as a perfect man, a perfect woman, or a perfect society made up of men and women. Such a thing as a perfect church, in which there are no weaknesses, no defective members, no faulty administrations, no backslidings, no unworthy people, does not exist. Some churches are much better and nearer right than others, but none are full up to the standard of perfection. In this world the Church is always and everywhere a mixed society, with mingled excellencies and faults. Even where the graces of the Spirit are the most active and the most fully developed, and people are most devoted and earnest, and the work of the Lord goes on with the greatest success, when the eye of the holy Jesus comes to survey the situation He always has plenty of occasion to say, "*Nevertheless, I have somewhat against thee.*"

And it is the same with individuals as with churches and congregations. We may think that we are all right, that we are doing nobly, that we have been very watchful, prayerful, true, devoted, and prompt in every known duty; but when Jesus comes to give His judgment, even while there is much for Him to commend and praise, He still in truth and justice must add, "*Nevertheless, I have somewhat against thee.*"

Nay, if we only look carefully into ourselves, our ways of living and doing, how we are handling ourselves, talents, possessions, hearts, and lives—how we are bearing and disposing ourselves respecting Christian duty and privilege, and what sort of progress we have been making in the divine life and usefulness,—we will be at no loss to find that Jesus, who knows and sees all, would needs have to say even of the best, "*Nevertheless, I have somewhat against thee.*"

The great fault Christ found with these people was the decay of their first love. They were good and earnest Christians still, but they had too much cooled in their ardor and let down in the fervency of their former zeal and devotion. There was still the outward ongoing of effort and activity, and much to be praised; but love was dying. The machinery still moved under the power of the original impulse, but the great moving spirit within was losing its force. The outside of the tree stood fair and well-proportioned as ever, but mould and decay had commenced within. A pure creed and a right discipline still remained, but the heart was growing cold. The Saviour saw how it was with them, and spoke accordingly.

And what, dear friends, does Christ's all-searching eye behold in us with reference to this point? Has there been no wane in our love and zeal since first we gave ourselves to Jesus? Are we as much interested in the things of God and the soul as once? Are we as prompt and earnest in our private devotions and attendance on the means of grace as aforetime? Do we have the same low opinion of the vanities, pursuits, honors, and pleasures of this world as when we first set out to serve the Lord? Are we as strict and particular in holding on to the truth or word of God, and as confident in venturing our trust and hopes upon it, as at some other time we could mention? Are we as devoted to the Church and as anxious and earnest and prayerful to build it up and to foster the spirit of peace, harmony, and love, as once? Ah me! in how many instances may awakened conscience catch the words of the loving Jesus, sadly whispering, "My child, my dear child, thou hast borne and hast patience for my name's sake, and hast labored, and hast not fainted. *Nevertheless, I have somewhat against thee!*"

Let us think on these things.

Lecture Second.

Rev. 2 : 5: "Remember therefore from whence thou art fallen, and repent, and do the first works; or else I will come unto thee quickly, and will remove thy candlestick out of his place, except thou repent."

WE have remarked upon the solemn fact that He who walks amid the golden candlesticks and whose eyes are like flames of fire sees and knows the works, character, and spiritual condition of all His churches and of every member in each. What is good, what is bad, what is improving and what is ailing, what is wanting and what is failing,—all is naked and open to His searching view, and no concealment can hide anything. If there is good, earnestness, and sincerity in any one, He notices that good and commends it.

There was much that was favorable in this church of Ephesus, and this is duly credited. But there were unfavorable symptoms also, and of a dangerous sort, and these are likewise pointed out for special attention and amendment, lest they should work ruin to the whole spiritual life of those concerned.

The particular defect was that these people had

"*left their first love.*" It is remarkable that this should happen in a church so eminent for its attainments, and standing at the head of all the churches of its time for activity, force, zeal, and devotion to the truth. Here was a congregation in which Paul had labored long and successfully, to which he had addressed an Epistle finding no cause for censure or evils to be corrected, over which Timothy had presided as chief pastor, and in the midst of which the beloved disciple dwelt in his later years, joining in its assemblies to the last, and often exhorting its members to faith and love. And yet it had so declined in spiritual life and devotion that Christ had to make this serious charge against it even while the apostle John still lived.

We thus see what a frail and fickle thing human nature is—how little dependence is to be placed upon it even at the best—how ineffectual the highest opportunities are to guarantee stability of religious character and devotion—how liable the most distinguished attainments to decay and disappear. Most of the same people who were in this church from the beginning were in it still, but it was now for the loving Saviour to say, "I have somewhat against thee, *because thou hast left thy first love.*"

These people were not in a state of apostasy. There still was much activity, zeal for evangelic truth, earnest adherence to apostolic order, hatred of error and unrighteousness, and regard for purity of life. But all this may exist, and yet a hidden canker be eating away what no orthodoxy, no faith, no knowledge, no good works, no labor or patience in well-doing could atone for. It was still a decent, orderly, vigorous, exemplary, and efficient church. Its external presentations were all good. But there was inward weakening in that very thing which is most essential—in that living love and fellowship of the soul with its Redeemer which is the life of all true piety. The body stood the same as before, but the mercury within had fallen. The machinery was still running, but the motive-power was failing. It was still the best of all the seven churches named, but it was at heart in a state of decline. Affection was cooling, zeal was abating. The inward fire of love was wasting away. A degeneration had set in which needed to be arrested and remedied.

These people still held firmly to the confession of the truth. They had religious knowledge and principle. They were true to what they had been taught, and held on commendably to it against all who encroached upon it either in doctrine or in life. They were still in many respects model Christians of the higher class. But the heart was not so deep in the matter as formerly. They could still withstand the terrors of persecution by the confidence and might of prayer, but those prayers had become less frequent, less ardent, and less confiding; their devotions more a matter of course than from inward desire to be in communion with Jesus; their religion more intellectual perhaps, but having less heart. They were still honored examples of the regenerating grace of God, and honored witnesses for the Gospel in the midst of a powerful heathenism; but the world had imperceptibly been insinuating itself between them and the Saviour, and, perhaps without knowing it themselves, they had lapsed from their first love.

Nor was this a peculiar or uncommon case. Too many Christians, alas! know from melancholy experience what it is to sink away from the fervors of a first devotion. Many can refer to times when they knew something of the happiness of entire consecration and full communion with Heaven—when the heart was withdrawn from everything temporal and fixed in undoubting faith upon Jesus—when they felt in the very newness and wonder of their emotions and resolves a proud confidence that nothing could ever remove them from an estate so blessed. But they have since found out how that life and joy could evaporate and pass away—how the care and love for other things insensibly stole in upon the soul, so that the bitter waters again filtered into their old channels, the chains again tightened upon the neck, and a drag formed upon the heart, until all former liberty and confidence was undermined, the old slavery renewed, and first love diminished and gone. Christ Himself has told us of some who hear the word, and anon with joy receive it, yet after a while lapse into their old folly and unconcern. Ah, dear friends, we know of too many such cases. We can point out numbers of them by name among ourselves. From the beginning the Saviour said it would be so. And such a frail and inconstant thing is human nature that I doubt if one of us has been without some experience of just what the Saviour here alleged against these Ephesians.

It is an easy thing to grow sluggish and indifferent in religious things, even when there has been a good and honest start and while there is no thought of backsliding. The truths once so bright and quickening to the soul are liable to become soiled by handling, and thus to lose their freshness and power. The natural heart, which still stirs within, is ever pleading for more liberal ideas and for less strictness than conscience at first so clearly dictated. The cares and anxieties of life make such heavy demands on our time and energy that religious duties are crowded into the background and punctuality in attending upon them is invaded and excused. Prayer and meditation on sacred things are narrowed to very feeble and uncertain limits. Bible reading and study become irregular and much hindered. Self-indulgence and carnal ease and pleasure sue for relaxation in the continual pressure which the burdens of business impose. A little yielding here and there seems to be necessary, and is so much more agreeable. And so, without intending it, and thinking all the while of keeping on good terms with conscience, people get upon the downward plane before they are aware of it, and finally awake, if they ever awake at all, to find themselves drifted far away from what they started to become and from what they once were. They have left their first love.

WHAT IS TO BE DONE IN SUCH A CASE?

The Saviour prescribed for these people of Ephesus, and what He said to them applies equally to ourselves. Truth is not a thing of one century, which becomes a cipher or a falsehood in the next, or which varies with latitude and longitude. Truth is like its God—the same yesterday, to-day, and for ever. What was truth at Ephesus is truth also in Philadelphia. Where the same disease exists, there the one and unchangeable remedy is requisite. And the word here spoken to the Christians of Ephesus is a leaf from the tree of life which needs to be applied in every case where love is dying.

The prescription given is made up of three items, and each of them of great importance.

The first item is, "*Remember therefore from whence thou art fallen.*" This calls for retrospection and the exercise of memory. True piety brings all our faculties into action. It is one of man's powers to be able to look back and to live the events and course of his life over again by means of memory. And this power is the first thing to be set to work to cure a decay of religious life and fervor. People must think back and compare what they once were with what they now are. Memory must recall the past that it may be laid alongside of the present.

When the apostle wished to bring the Jewish Christians to a firm and continuous steadfastness in the faith, he bade them "call to remembrance the former days, in which, after they were illuminated, they endured a great fight of afflictions, and took joyfully the spoiling of their goods, knowing that they had in heaven a better and more enduring substance" (Heb. 10: 32). The Saviour did the same with reference to these people of the church of Ephesus; and so it must be with us all.

Consult your memory, then, as to how it was with you aforetime. Call to mind how it was when you made your first start in Christianity—what adoring love and gratitude you felt toward the merciful Saviour who snatched you as a brand from the burning—what fervor, what zeal, what earnestness of devotion, distinguished your feelings by day and were as the sunlight around your soul at night—how prompt and ready you were for any duty and any sacrifice by which you could honor and glorify your blessed Lord—how precious to you was the word of your God as you read and marked its glowing texts or listened to it from the sacred desk as often as Sunday came—how the psalms and hymns and spiritual songs of the Church reverberated in your soul, and what melody to the Lord they made in your heart—how easy and free and frequent were your communings with God, and what confidence you had in the forgiving love and favor of the heavenly Father—to what a paradise of peace and satisfaction grace raised you, on what sunlit summits you then walked in sweet communion with Him whose redeeming love you had learned to know and feel, and with what disdain and loathing you thence looked down upon the empty husks and baubles of worldly gayety and carnal pleasuring as compared with the high things then so near and dear to your soul. And as you trace the glowing picture, still bright on the tablets of memory, think of how it is with you now. Do those halcyon days still shine upon your path, filling your soul with their supernal brightness? Do you still find yourself aloft, triumphing upon the Rock of Ages and breathing joyously the pure atmosphere of God's heavens? Or has there been a change, interposing a wide gulf between that blessed past and this present? Are you conscious of some mysterious difference for the worse? Have sighs for the joys you have tasted come into the place of those happy songs? Has cold and chill and cloud and dimness and darkness and doubt and heaviness quenched out that ardent warmth of joy in the Lord and pleasure in His service? Make the comparison and see if there has been no unfavorable transition.

I do not say that the enthusiasm of first discipleship will or must always gush and spring as at the beginning. Youthful emotions naturally and necessarily sober down amid the realities of afterlife, and so religious enthusiasm and ecstasies as well; but then they must settle into deeper principle. An old Christian may have less passion than at his entrance on the heavenly way, but the spring of religious character and devotion must still be there, all the steadier and firmer for the growth of years, ready on occasion joyfully to make sacrifices for Christ, and as appreciative of all that belongs to the nurture and exercises of Christian life as ever. The first glow of early feeling may be sobered down, but what is lost in fervor must be regained in fixedness, depth, and strength, the energy of principle acting in the room of the enthusiasm of feeling when life was younger. Though there may be less effervescence to incite and impel, there must be settled conviction and tried purpose to move one forward all the same and with all the more steadiness. There may not be as much rampage of religious emotion and joy, but the living principle must be there to act out duty as the crisis for it comes. The leaping, dancing, and sparkling rill may lose its dash and hurry, but only to widen and deepen into the calm majesty of the river, the latter still moving steadily on to the same great ocean toward which the other bounded with so much life. Otherwise, there is unwholesome stagnation, and first love is dying out, if not already dead.

It may be unpleasant to recall a joyous past in comparison with a sad and faulty present. It is no comforting discovery to find that we have been retrograding and going down hill instead of up. But we need to know the facts if there is to be an effectual remedy. Jesus tells us to make this retrospect as the first step to a reparation of the lapse that has intervened. And why should we try to hide from ourselves what we cannot hide from our Saviour, and what must work death to all our hopes if not discovered and vigorously treated? If we have been losing our first love, we need to know it, and trying to conceal it from ourselves will not relieve the misfortune. Therefore the word of the merciful Saviour is, "*Remember from whence thou art fallen.*" The facts must be considered.

And the next step is equally clear. One word expresses it: they that have left their first love must "*repent.*" They must confess the evil, be sorry for it, and set earnestly to work to retrace their steps, in order to get back into the true life of faith. When Peter stood convicted of having wickedly denied his Lord, he did not try to hide it from his soul or to apologize for it as a thing which he was betrayed into and could not help. No; he knew that he was a sinner; he felt it in his soul. It wounded and distressed him that he should have made himself answerable for so great a piece of cowardice and wickedness toward his meek and suffering Lord. And he "*went out and wept bitterly.*" Broken-hearted for his terrible fall, he threw himself on the mercy of God, and with a soul aching with abhorrence of his crime, and thoroughly changed from any further fellowship with his sin, he sued for pardon. His broken heart was already a reinstatement, in so far as it carried with it an altered mind and a renewed devotion to his Lord. This was his repentance, and it was effectual. And so are we to repent of our fall from first love. We must not apologize for it; we must not try to hide it from us; we must not begin to think that we could not help it; but must own up to ourselves and to God, with wounded and sorrowing hearts, that we have been so faithless and untrue, humbly imploring restoration to His favor, and made up to leave nothing undone to be cured and healed of our guilty defection, and by His good help henceforth to keep ourselves in His love.

Not all repentance is the same. There is a repentance which looks at the consequences and punishments of sin, and struggles simply to escape from them; and there is a repentance which looks at the guilt and wrong of sin, and sorrows over it for its evilness, and struggles for deliverance from it because of its meanness and hatefulness. We see the one kind in Pharaoh, who cried, *"Take away the frogs,"* which his wickedness had brought upon him and his country. We see the other in David, who cried, *"Take away my sin;* wash me from mine iniquity; purge me with hyssop, and I shall be clean; create in me a clean heart, O God, and renew a right spirit within me." The one drives to despair, as in the case of Judas; the other leads back, in broken-hearted return, to wronged Goodness, saying, "Father, I have sinned before heaven and in thy sight, and am no more worthy to be called thy son," as in the case of the Prodigal.

There is also a repentance which expresses great sorrow for sin to-day while the penalties of transgression are sore and heavy, but when the pain is over is ready to plunge again into the same misdoings. This was the sort that appeared so often in King Saul, but which failed to make a right man of him or to save him from the doom of a guilty and rejected suicide. The repentance which the Saviour calls for in the text is a repentance that confesses and laments sin because it is sin, and sorrows for having given place to what is so wrong, evil, hurtful, and offensive, and is honestly desirous and resolved to amend. And not until we come to this are we in the right way to heal and repair the evil of having fallen from our first love.

And yet there remains one other item in the prescription. Remembering whence we have fallen, and sincerely repenting, it belongs to the proceeding for the backslider to re-begin his whole Christian life. "*Do the first works*" is the direction the blessed Saviour gives. This means the setting of ourselves upon the same path and in the same way in which we came to our first love. It does not mean that we must be rebaptized, but that we must come back to our baptism, to the meaning of it—to the consecration to Christ of which it is the mark and badge—to the covenant and promises of which it is the divine seal. It does not mean that we must be reconfirmed; but that we must come back again to precisely the same point of renunciation of the devil and all his works, the vanities of the world, and the sinful desires of the flesh—to renewal of faith in God and in His Son our Saviour, sincerely desiring to be received into the fellowship and liberty of His true children—to the unreserved surrender of ourselves, hearts, and lives to the loving obedience of faith, to live and die as the willing subjects and followers of Him in whom our salvation stands. Confessing and lamenting our past failures, grieved in soul that we could ever slacken and sink away in our affection and devotion to so true and good a Lord, feeling and sorrowing for our unworthiness and ill-desert, full of earnest longings and prayers for God's merciful forgiveness, and honestly desiring by His gracious help to be and do and suffer whatever His holy will may be,—so are we to come to Him, as we came at the first, throwing ourselves on His compassion, and in all the depths of our nature, saying,

> Here, Lord, I give myself to Thee,
> 'Tis all that I can do.

By all the powers a gracious God has given us

and will give we must reform from all neglects, from all dalliance with the ways of the world, from all half-heartedness in religion. This is doing the first works over again, even those which gave us those better days, the holy music of which still comes up in memory amid all the cold and wretchedness of the estrangement which has since befallen us. And nothing less than this can bring about a return of that spiritual summertime or repair the mischief of having left our first love. Indeed, this is what God calls for from all people, at all times, if they would enjoy His peace.

Happily, however, we have many hopeful encouragements to all this. Backsliders know to what heights of peace and holy joy they once were lifted by the grace in which they then hoped and trusted; and that grace is the same now and able to do for us the same again. Jesus sends His special message, bidding those who have left their first love to remember whence they have fallen, repent, and do the first works; and He would not give such a prescription if it were not a competent remedy to work a complete cure. Many of the ancient saints, when fallen into such spiritual decay, tried it and found themselves once more peaceful and happy in the love and favor of Heaven. And God's word and promises on the subject are plentiful, clear, and most encouraging.

Of old time He said to Jeremiah, "Go and proclaim these words, and say, Return, thou backsliding Israel, saith the Lord; and I will not cause mine anger to fall upon you; for I am merciful" (Jer. 3:12). By Isaiah He has given out, "Let the wicked forsake his way, and the unrighteous man his thoughts, and let him return unto the Lord, and He will have mercy upon him" (Isa. 55:7). By Hosea the word is, "O Israel, return unto the Lord thy God," with promise: "I will heal their backsliding, I will love them freely" (Hos. 14:1–4). Jesus Himself saith, "Come unto Me, all ye that labor and are heavy laden, and I will give you rest" (Matt. 11:28). Nor can there be any question that in returning and humble resting in Jesus we shall be saved; for so the voice of the whole Scripture is.

And yet we must not overlook the fact that there is also an awful threat in the text in case Christ's lapsed and faulty children do not repent and return as He directs. To such He says He will come quickly and remove their candlestick, turning the light of mercy into the darkness of judgment, and the greatness of their privileges to a millstone to sink them beyond all hope.

See how it was with the church of Ephesus. Its improvement was but temporary. It decaye still more with the general decay that came afterward. No great length of time passed until a visitor there might well have asked if the lightnings of divine vengeance had wrought the desolations that were upon that ill-fated city. And for these long ages since, the melancholy echoes from the crumbling walls and fallen temples of a lost Christianity have been answering back, "Look on us, and see what Jesus means by the removal of the candlestick from its place."

Lecture Third.

Rev. 2 : 7 : "He that hath an ear, let him hear what the Spirit saith unto the churches; To him that overcometh will I give to eat of the tree of life, which is in the midst of the paradise of God."

THE intensity and the directness to every one of the exhortation in the first part of this text bespeak the presence of truths of great importance. It has been rightly said that "this form always is used of radical and generative truths, great principles, most precious promises, most deep fetches from the secrets of God, being as it were eyes of truth, seeds and kernels of knowledge"—things in which mankind have the profoundest interest, and without the learning of which we are at great disadvantage. By these words, then, appended as they are to each of these seven Letters, we are here instructed by the Saviour Himself that they are of very momentous import and relate to things of the deepest consequence to our welfare.

But the same words also propound a matter of urgent duty which we are not at liberty to omit or disregard. The Scriptures everywhere make much of *hearing*—the giving of attention to what God has been pleased to record and make known to us in His word. When Jehovah speaks it is for those to whom He speaks to give ear and to observe what He says. When He calls to us and makes communications it is for us to regard and consider what He speaks. He who walks in the midst of the golden candlesticks does not dictate Letters to His churches and send them to us from heaven, and yet leave it to our whims or option to give attention to them or not. Giving us these utterances of His mind and judgment, He gives with them His solemn command and requirement: *"He that hath an ear, let him hear what the Spirit saith unto the churches."*

First of all, we then have here a solemn rebuke to those who call themselves Christians, and yet seldom if ever look into their Bibles to read and study them, and do not seem to care what the Holy Ghost has spoken. Though the Scriptures are given to be to us our light and guide in making our way through this dark world, many so-called Christian people do not care for the reading of the word or whether they attend upon the preaching of it or not. Some think they have fulfilled their duty if they read a text now and then, and hear a sermon once a week when the weather is inviting or when they do not know what else to do with themselves of a Sunday. Having ears to hear, it is the Saviour's command to us to "hear what the Spirit saith;" but few is the number who care to obey it.

And when we come to a close comparison of the divine precepts with the ways in which many treat God's holy word, we cannot but wonder at His forbearance toward the great mass of those who make up our modern Christendom. With all the activities and zeal of these people of Ephesus, the Saviour still found occasion to fault them with having left their first love; but when we look at most of the church-people of our day, even in regard to this one item of "hearing what the Spirit saith," it would seem very doubtful if they ever had any real love at all. It becomes every one of us, therefore, to search and try ourselves well as to our treatment and hearing of what God has given for our learning, that through patience and comfort of the Scriptures we may have hope.

Nor should we forget the fact that everything touching our salvation depends on the giving of an attentive ear to the divine word and the diligent use of our privileges, to hear, mark, learn, and inwardly digest what it contains. Jesus prayed for His followers: "Sanctify them by Thy truth, Thy word is truth;" but how can the word sanctify us if we do not hear it and are not concerned to know and understand it? It is written that "Whosoever shall call upon the name of the Lord shall be saved;" but "How shall they call on Him in whom they have not believed? and how shall they believe in Him of whom they have not *heard?*" Hearing and right learning of the word lie at the basis of everything. If there is no proper hearing, there can be no right believing; and where no right faith is there can be no salvation. It is therefore in itself a most vital thing that, having ears, we should use them to hear and learn all the word and communications of God, as Jesus Himself here lays it upon every one to do.

But this exhortation has also a deeper meaning. Every one has capacity to give attention, and so it is laid upon every one to employ that capacity. But not every one who hears with the outward ear does thereby really hear in the full sense of the Saviour's meaning. There is an inward hearing—a hearing in which the things spoken take hold on the soul and inform and move it—a hearing which answers to what is heard. There must be spiritual discernment, a taking in of the truth, and a heart-heeding of it, so as to be guided, influenced, and controlled by it in our thinking and doing.

There are people spoken of in the Scriptures as "uncircumcised in heart and ears," to whom the word is only as a pleasant sound which takes no hold to shape character or affect the life. The truth is, that a right-hearing ear in sacred things is a gift of God and a matter of grace. It is a spiritual organ which only the Holy Ghost can create—a spiritual sense which God must awaken. Hence, also, if any one has not such a spiritual ear, his duty is to seek the grace by which he may have it, and inwardly hear, so as to become a *doer* of the work. It is a grace which God is ever ready and pleased to give to every one sincerely desirous to possess it or who wishes savingly to learn His truth. Nay, the power to create it is in the word itself, which is so constituted and inwrought with the energy of the Spirit that it will create its own way to an effectual hearing if people will only entertain it and listen to it with a view to learn and obey it. "The word of God is quick and powerful, sharper than any two-edged sword;" and if people will only receive it into "good and honest hearts," willing and anxious to be profited by it, its quickening power will be realized and fruit abundant will come of it. And, as the Saviour calls upon us to hear to good practical purpose, He at the same time makes it our duty to set ourselves with devout desire and prayerfulness rightly to hear and to be conformed to His word. Some hear but little, yet learn much, while others hear much, yet learn but little; and the whole difference lies in the earnestness or unconcern with which people hear or try to learn the truth.

Nor should we fail to notice in passing that He who dictates these Letters to the churches, and is Himself the speaker throughout, yet calls them "*what the Spirit saith.*" He thus asserts an absolute identity between His doing and the Spirit's doing in the giving of the word. He would have us see and know that what He says the Holy Ghost says, and that what the Spirit says, that He says. The Holy Ghost is the Spirit of the Son, the same as of the Father; and so the Son is one in the same Trinity with both. What the Father doeth, that doeth the Son likewise; and what the Son saith is at the same time what the Spirit saith. What is here spoken is therefore in every sense and respect the absolute word of God, even the Triune God, which is sufficient reason why every one that hath an ear should hear.

Notice, then, the character and attitude of those who become true hearers of the divine word.

A great promise is here given. The word is that "*to him that overcometh*" great rewards are in reserve. To overcome implies conflict. It bespeaks enemies, antagonisms, and opposing hindrances. We cannot speak of victory where there has been no contest, no enemies to conquer, no difficulties to surmount. And as the promise is "to him that *overcometh*," the idea is that every right hearer of the word is a combatant—one who has to contend with enemies and opposition—one who has the character and attitude of a fighter—one who has to make his way by conflict.

It is a marked truth that as people become living Christians they become *soldiers*. This lies in the very nature of things, and cannot be otherwise, whether we like it or not. No one can reach heaven without fighting his way through an enemy's country. This world lieth in the wicked one. Satan is its prince and master. His dominion is indeed a usurpation which must eventually be destroyed, but for the present it holds. The great mass of this world's population is under Satan's sway. He rules in the children of disobedience. And under his kingdom we all are born, having the taint of his depravity upon us from our very coming into the world. In becoming Christians we take another Lord, come under a new rule, enlist under another standard, and set up rebellion against the dominion of the Evil One; and so we are at once thrown into conflict with Satan's empire, and must contend and fight to maintain ourselves and come off victorious.

One thing we have to contend with is *ignorance*—spiritual darkness. The reason why many are so easy in their sinfulness, poverty, and danger is that they do not know their real condition. Their moral perceptions are darkened, their spiritual vision is obscured and perverted; they have no understanding of the situation. And it is hard to get men's eyes open to the facts. People have to learn of God, of truth, of Christ, of the reality of spiritual things, of the destitution and needs of the soul, and of the way of life. So many false impressions and miserable deceptions and lying persuasions have to be found out, conquered, and put aside that a true man is in perpetual conflict and effort to come to a knowledge of the truth and to get hold of the only safe and saving wisdom.

Another thing to be fought is *our carnal nature*, with its many lusts warring against the soul. We are ever prone to be influenced most by what meets and gratifies the earthly senses and pleases our sensuous imagination. Many live only for the body and what pertains to the ease and glory of the earthly man. "The lusts of the flesh, and lusts of the eyes, and the pride of life" have wonderful power in all of us to control, enlist, and absorb our affections and activities, to the exclusion of spiritual and eternal things, which lie beyond the reach of our earthly senses. They are very potent to crowd God out of our thoughts. He who would be a right man has thus continually to fight against this tendency or be drawn along in a way to starve and ruin his immortal nature. It takes effort, watching, and ever-renewed endeavor to keep alive to an unseen world, to endure as seeing Him who is invisible, and to be duly anxious about spiritual bread and good-fortune. Beset as we are in this world with the pressing claims and flattering promises of worldly good and pleasure, it requires a strong and perpetual fight to be successful in keeping ourselves in the love and service of God. When it comes to a question between a fortune and a dishonesty —between a fleshly delight and a religious duty —between honorable standing in the eyes of men and strict obedience to the clear commands of God—between our ease, likes, or fancies, and Gospel requirements—between plenty, happiness, and comfort in this world and self-denial and suffering for the rewards of eternity—between an inviting lie and a humiliating truth—between money hoarded for the love of it and money to be parted with to answer God's calls—between promotion on earth and humble fidelity to the Lord Jesus,—the decision is not so easy, and multitudes take the wrong side and are led captive by the devil's power. Duty and selfishness, faith and unbelief, the new man and the old, are ever wrestling and contending with each other in every one honestly desiring to maintain a Christian life. Paul felt this struggle, and tells us of a law in his members warring against the law of his mind, and exclaims over the wretchedness often induced by the fact that when he would do good evil was present with him.

And with all these things are *the subtle activities of Satan* and his evil confederates. These constitute an unseen, malignant, and multitudinous host of spiritual agencies and powers in league to defeat the gracious will of God. From them come all sorts of cunning machinations and assaults which have to be encountered and overcome. In the garb of the best of friends, and often transforming themselves into angels of light, they obtrude themselves to deceive and lead astray, inject upon our minds every variety of insinuations and ill promptings, ever trying to persuade us that evil is good and good evil, and imposing upon multitudes of unsuspecting souls. We are told that Satan goeth about, through his various emissaries, as a roaring lion, seeking whom he may devour. Paul assures us that our fight and warfare are not only with flesh and blood, but with principalities and powers, the rulers in the darkness of this world and wicked spirits in the air. They can do us no mischief if we are firm in resisting them, and use the means of withstanding them, and keep on the alert against being betrayed into their power; but it demands constant vigilance, effort, and many sharp conflicts to resist and vanquish them and their cunning devices. They have many agents in this world to solicit, tempt, and influence us against the truth, to try to laugh us out of faith in the Gospel and the duties of piety, and by false science and a show of superior wisdom to undermine our confidence. And in one way or another we constantly have to contend with these unclean spirits.

These enemies we are obliged to withstand, resist, and conquer, or they will conquer us. Enlisting under Christ's banner, we enter upon a war, and cannot come out of it but as victors or vanquished. It is often a very trying war, but the helps are ample, and success is sure if we are only vigilant, courageous, and true; and grand rewards await him who "overcometh."

To encourage and strengthen us in this strife the Saviour here says to each and every one, *"To him that overcometh will I give to eat of the tree of life which is in the midst of the paradise of God."* Beautiful promise! and as rich in significance as it is in beauty.

What all is meant by "the tree of life" we cannot fully explain. We first read of it in the happy beginning of our world, when man was innocent and Eden was his home and God was his familiar friend. Jehovah planted it. It was "in the midst of the garden" as the central ornament and the most blessed product of that abode of blessedness. The eating of the fruit of it in the primeval Paradise seems to have been meant as a sacrament of fellowship with life—a pledge, support, and appropriation of life eternal for soul and body.

There was once much sacredness in eating, though there is so much sin connected with it now; and when redemption once comes to its completion that sacred eating is to be restored. If saints in glory do not need to eat, they can eat; and as the fall came by eating disobediently, and for it man has ever since been excluded from the tree having sublimest virtue, so redemption is to bring man once more within reach of that tree to eat of its blest fruits. Paradise restored is the tree of life restored, and man redeemed is to find it one of the happiest features of his immortality that he shall be given to eat of that tree. Sin cut us off from it, and the victory of faith in the Son of God is to bring us back to it and it to us. There will be neither hunger nor thirst in heaven, nor are we to suppose that there will be any waste in the energies of the glorified calling for recuperation by means of corporeal digestion; but still, there will be some kind of eating there—eating of the fruits of the tree of life—some deep communion with Life, constituting one of the highest joys of eternity.

Very much is said about Life in connection with the rewards of the saints. "Eternal Life"

—"everlasting Life"—"entrance into Life"—"a crown of Life"—"the river of Life"—"the tree of Life," are everywhere most hopefully and joyously spoken of. Even for Christians in this world we read of "the bread of Life"—"the water of Life"—"the Spirit of Life"—"the grace of Life"—"the savor of Life unto Life"—"the power of Life"—"the word of Life." Wisdom, as commended in the book of Proverbs, is said to be "a tree of Life to them that lay hold on her." It is said that "the fruit of righteousness is a tree of Life." And, like the golden table of showbread which ever stood in the ancient tabernacle and temple for the priests, so the Tree of Life stands in all the golden street-way of the New Jerusalem with monthly fruits for the immortal ones in glory, to which all that have washed their robes have free and unlimited access.

What all this may mean is more than we can conceive, but privilege and blessedness unspeakable are indicated. There is a heavenly Paradise. The presence of God is there. It is luminous with the glory of God and the Lamb. Nothing false or unclean or unsavory can ever enter it. It is the everlasting home-place of the saints. Its foundations are jewels. Its walks are gold. Its watchmen are angels. It is the metropolis of intensest, highest, purest, and holiest *Life*. Its rivers are rivers of Life. Its trees are trees of Life. Its waters are waters of Life. Its inhabitants are those who have eternal Life and have entered into Life, and inherit ever more and more of everlasting Life. And this is the lot and portion which the blessed Saviour here engages to give to him that overcometh.

The promise to the victor also corresponds to the ill to be vanquished. These Ephesians were wasting and failing in their first love. Their spiritual life was beginning to yield and weaken. There was danger that they would lose the vital energy of religious devotion. They were growing faint and flabby in the life of faith. This weakening and downwardness they were now called on to resist and fight and overcome. And the promise to the victor is in the line of the trouble they were to combat. They were becoming inwardly weak, therefore there was promise of spiritual nourishment. There was decay of life, and so there was promise of the highest and most plenteous food of life. For a wasting state they were to have Paradise. For their weakening in the springs of life they were to have to eat of the Tree of Life.

The special rewards of the victorious always take their intensest form from the sort of work done or the particular kind of trouble and adversity conquered and surmounted. The Ephesians were fainting in the fervency of love and the energy of spirituality, and they were pointed to the Tree of Life in the midst of the Paradise of God. The Smyrniotes were in great trial of persecution, under which many yielded up their lives as martyrs, and they were pointed to exemption from the second death. And so in each instance the kind of weakness and trouble to be overcome reappears in the peculiarity of the promise to the victor, and those who conquer in their contest with the worst have the highest reward.

But we must not overlook the individuality of this promise. It is not made to the church as a body, but to each separate member of it: "To *him* that overcometh." Jesus well knew that the earthly church, as such, would never overcome, and that there never would be a church made up of none but overcomers. But He knew also that in the faultiest churches there are still some true and faithful ones to maintain the fight unto final victory. Hence the promise is to the individual members.

It is not the general fight of the Church against the world that is here in view, but the individual fight of each soul with the errors, weaknesses, and faults that are around us, in the Church as well as out of it. Let the Church, as such, be and do as it will; we are not to look so much to it as to ourselves—not to what others may be and do, but to what we are. The Church cannot hear, believe, and love for us, nor repent for us, nor overcome for us; we must each hear, believe, love, and overcome for ourselves. The Church, as it appears on earth as a whole, cannot hope to be admitted to the Tree of Life. It embraces too many faulty members for that. But as individuals we may indulge this hope if we struggle on in faith. We can never hope that this our Church of the Holy Communion, or any other church, shall ultimately appear as a body in Paradise; but we dare hope, blessed be God! that we as individual members may appear there. And to us as individuals the promise is that if we only hold on, work on, pray on, and exert ourselves in the diligent use of the grace given us, and press our warfare to final victory, Jesus will give us place and reward according to the trials we have withstood, the weaknesses we have overcome, the victories over self and sin and error we have won.

Ah yes, dear friends, though Sodom blazes behind us, Jerusalem's gates of pearl stand open in our front. Whatever desolations of once-glorious churches, dissolving of cities, perishing of states, or crumbling of thrones under Jehovah's judgments may come to pass, our home is Paradise, our food the fruit of the Tree of Life, if only we fight on to victory. And in that immortal retreat of peace and purity and love no wintry cloud shall come to cast its chilling shadow on us, no hurricane or earthquake uproot the place of our rest, no lightning's blast or tornado scathe or enemy assail; for our life shall be in full fellowship with its Source, never more to be severed from the food that nourishes it to the fulness of its being and blessedness.

> All hopes, all wishes, all the love
>   We sighed for, pined for, ever,
> Shall bloom around us there above,
>   And last with us for ever.

Lecture Fourth.

Rev. 2:8-11: "And unto the angel of the church in Smyrna, write: These things saith the first and the last, which was dead, and is alive; I know thy works, and tribulation, and poverty (but thou art rich), and I know the blasphemy of them which say they are Jews, and are not, but are the synagogue of Satan. Fear none of those things which thou shalt suffer. Behold, the devil shall cast some of you into prison, that ye may be tried; and ye shall have tribulation ten days. Be thou faithful unto death, and I will give thee a crown of life. He that hath an ear, let him hear what the Spirit saith unto the churches: He that overcometh shall not be hurt of the second death."

OF the seven churches this in Smyrna was the most afflicted and oppressed. It was poor; it was much reviled by false pretenders; it was sorely persecuted. Satan's malignity seemed to have taken on special fierceness against it, casting some of its members into prison and raising fiery storms against its venerable pastor, the holy Polycarp. The church of Ephesus was in peril from inward weakening and the decay of love, but the church of Smyrna was in peril from its external enemies and the afflictions that were upon it from without. And to this state of sorrow and suffering the Saviour chiefly speaks in this Letter.

Already in the superscription He describes Himself in the way best fitted to comfort and establish them against the afflictions they were in. It is not His walking in the midst of the golden candlesticks, and His holding of the seven stars in His right hand, that He here puts forward, but His being the First and the Last, His having died and yet being alive again, and living for ever. He thus proclaimed Himself to their confidence as older, mightier, and more enduring than the persons and powers which were oppressing them—as having gone through similar experiences Himself, and hence able to sympathize with their griefs—as having gloriously triumphed and risen to blessed immortality notwithstanding that He suffered and died—as being indeed just such a Lord and Saviour as they needed to keep them amid their tribulations and bring them through to final glory and blessedness.

It is something for poor sufferers to know that they have some one in whom to trust who is qualified to master the case; that it is not in an arm of flesh they hope; that He whom they look to as their Saviour is the same who saw the stars kindle and suns bud into being, and who will live on in the same unwaning life and majesty should stars and suns expire and all material creations be changed like a wornout garment. Nay more, that while His hands propel the worlds in their circuits He wears the nature of a brother-man, and has a heart that beats in sympathy with every pang in ours; that He Himself has gone through heavier sorrows and a far deeper death than any that can ever come upon His believing followers; that He bears with Him upon His heavenly throne the thorn-marks and the nail-prints to keep alive His tenderness and consideration for His sorrowing people on earth, still struggling with tribulation and death for His name's sake; and that in the power of an endless life He ever lives, the imperishable vanquisher of all the potencies of death and hell. Thus the blessed Lord Jesus presented Himself to these suffering saints at Smyrna, as also to all His people, in their trials.

Very tenderly also does He speak: "*I know thy works.*" These works were neither many nor great. The people were too poor, too oppressed, too feeble and afflicted, to do any great things. But the smallness of their works did not exclude them from the loving Saviour's regard. He notices the mite of the widow as well as the costly donations of the rich. He estimates men according to the grace in the heart, and not according to the strength in the hand. He does not look so much at the brilliancy of our deeds as at the cheerful willingness of the soul to do what it can. Not the greatness of the outward achievement, but the inward principle of devoted love, is what He considers.

Great things are expected of those who have ten talents, and it will be all the worse for them if their works do not come up to their ability; but the faithful employment of one talent, if that be all we have, though the results may count little or nothing in men's esteem, is as great and precious to the heart of Jesus as the more showy works of the rich and mighty. The penny of the little child and the prayers of the helpless invalid are as dear to Jesus and rise as high in heaven as the thousands and thousands of the millionnaire or the achievements of the Church's strongest champions. When people have it not in their power to do, and yet with earnest and devoted heart do what they can, and out of their weakness and penury show that the living power of grace is in them, even their little works rise like incense to the skies and have their record in the notice and commendation of our Lord equally with the greater things of those who possess superior ability. To the poorest and the weakest, as well as to the richest and the strongest, the Saviour says, "*I know thy works.*" And whether we do much or little, exert ourselves to the full stretch of our ability or lag behind in what we might readily achieve, we need never think that our Lord and Judge is not taking note of it, or that He does not take full measure of it according to what is in our power and what is not.

But Jesus not only took knowledge of the "*works*" of this poor church, but also of its afflicted estate. "*I know thy tribulation and poverty*," says He; and a whole volume of grace and tenderness was in those words.

Christian suffering, like Christian rejoicing, is something of a mystery to the world. The carnal mind cannot understand it, and takes little or no account of it. The world does not at all enter into a Christian's experience or a Christian's tribulation. A true child of God grieves over things which the world cares nothing for, and rejoices in things in which the world sees no happiness. As John wrote, so it is ever: "The world knoweth us not, because it knew Him not." But our Saviour knoweth—"*I know thy tribulation.*" Not as a spy, not as an inquisitor, not in the cold omniscience of one who knows everything, but as the head knows the hurt that has befallen some member of the body—as a mother contemplates the suffering of her darling child—as a generous heart enters into the misfortunes of his near and dear friend,—so does Jesus know our tribulation. He knows it not only with the head, but with the heart.

He knows it as a thing which He Himself has either sent or permitted. Nothing can happen without Him who is "head over all things to the Church." There is no such thing as chance—no fortuitous concourse of things to affect and shape destiny without amenability to the all-governing power now lodged in the hands of Jesus. No tribulation can come to a Christian—no headache or heartache, no fever or consumption, no loss of fortune or treachery of friends, no bereavement, no persecution, no weakness, no poverty, no days of darkness or temptation, no distress of body or sorrow of soul—but as Jesus wills, appoints, or allows. We may often lose sight of the fact, but it is the fact all the same, that never a woe falls upon us which has not first been in the wise consideration and beneficent bosom of our blessed Lord and Saviour. It had to receive its commission from His loving heart before it could touch us. He therefore knows our tribulation, and knows it far better than we ourselves.

He also knows the need and use of it. He might prevent it if He would, but that might not be the best. It would not be well for us if we were never afflicted, never disappointed, never crossed or troubled in our passage through this world. Uninterrupted prosperity would be serious misfortune to a Christian. There is "a needs be" that trial and suffering should come to discipline and soften us. A hurt child thinks of its parent, and hastens to that parent with its misfortune, and is all the more loving and devoted when properly rebuked and chastised for its errors and wrong-doings; and we need similar experience, that we may remember whose we are and where to find our true help and comfort. Each heart knows its own sorrows best, but, whatever the grief, there is some moral and spiritual need for it. However inexplicable to us, Jesus understands it, and knows what it is to do for us and what the mischief would be without it.

It is necessary that there should be sickness, bereavements, losses, reverses, disappointments, and sufferings for us in this world. They go along with Christ's sufferings to fulfil an important office in helping us to our better destiny. Afflictions and trials are some of the links in the chain which is to lift us to true faith and trust in God, and which cannot be dispensed with until we come to the heavenly kingdom, where such discipline is no more needed. Like surgical operations to save the life of the body, so earthly afflictions are to aid in saving the life of the soul. Our heavenly Physician knows this, and hence does not exempt us from sharp, disabling, and bitter pains and sorrowful experiences here on earth. A true believer is always made better by suffering, and can often reach and accomplish through his adversities what could not have been without them. And, whatever the tribulation,

Jesus knows it and has weighed all the purposes of goodness and grace for which it is sent or permitted.

It is a hard thing to suffer and to be always exposed to the buffetings and ills of this world; but it is also a precious thing if we did but see it in all its bearings and effects. Darkness is repulsive, but we need it in order to see the beauty of the stars. I doubt not that the redeemed in heaven will as earnestly thank the Lord for what they suffer here as for their days of peace, health, and sunshine. Heaven will be all the sweeter and more enjoyable for the sorrows of the way through which it has been reached. Myriads will be there at last who never would have reached that blessed world but for the tribulations they experienced on earth. All this is plain to our blessed Saviour's eyes, and hence He does not exempt us from earthly trials.

But He also knows our tribulation to sympathize with us in it. It is as painful to a loving parent to chastise an erring child as it is for the child; and we may be sure that Jesus has no pleasure in the pains and trials which yet are so needful for us. Not a pang goes through the heart of a child of God but it also goes through the heart of Christ. Whatsoever is done to the least of these He takes as done unto Himself. Christians are members of His body, of His flesh, and of

His bones; and when they are hurt He feels it even upon His throne, "for we have not an high priest which cannot be touched with the feeling of our infirmity." He has been through the fires and knows the pains they give, and He is not unmoved as He sees His people writhing in the scorching flames. He sits by the crucible like a refiner of silver, intensely watching the precious metal while he directs and fans the fires, looking to see His own image reflected in the shining mass that He may then quickly deliver it from the burning. Not one pang or moment more in fire than is needed to this end will He allow; and during all the process His loving eyes and anxious heart are with the sufferer in the trying pains. What necessity requires Him to appoint He softens by His sympathizing tenderness. However lowly and poor and neglected and forgotten the suffering child of God may be, there is an electric cord between it and Him. Nothing can happen to us here that is not at the same time before His presence in heaven. He knows our tribulation and our poverty—knows it to feel for us and to sustain and comfort us in it and to direct it to our greater glory in the end.

These people of Smyrna were great sufferers. A powerful class of men, claiming to be the representatives of the only true religion, did all they could to bring them into contempt and disgrace.

The heathen were very adverse to them. They were enduring much, and were to encounter still severer woes. By the malignity of their enemies some of them were to be cast into prison, others to die as martyrs, and fearful trial was to be upon them all. Polycarp, the friend and disciple of St. John, was then their venerable pastor. For many long years he had labored and suffered with them. But he was to be taken from them and burned alive because he would not deny Christ and abjure allegiance to the Saviour whom he served and preached.

An account of the martyrdom of this noble man has come down to us. Dragged before the Roman proconsul, he was promised liberty if only he would abjure Christ, but his answer was, "Eighty-and-six years have I served Him, and He hath never wronged me; and how can I blaspheme my King, who hath saved me?" At this touching confession Jews and heathen alike clamored to have him burnt alive, and hurried to gather the fuel for the purpose. When they were about to fasten him to the stake he bade them spare their nails—that God would keep him steadfast in the fires without the need of such fastenings; and counted it a blessedness to be thought worthy of a place among the martyrs of Jesus. And even amid the fires which consumed his mortal body he was heard singing and praising God and blessing the name of His Son Jesus Christ. He was "the angel" of the church to whom the word was, "Fear none of those things which thou shalt suffer. Be faithful unto death and I will give thee a crown of life." And this is the way the holy man fulfilled the divine directions.

We know not, dear friends, what awaits us in the future. We only know that in this world we shall have tribulation. Our calling in Christ Jesus necessarily leads through suffering and trial. It may be lighter to some and heavier to others; "but what son is he whom the Father chasteneth not?" It is well that our eyes are holden from what the chastisement is to be, lest we should be unfitted for present duty; but we may well believe that the brightest home and the happiest heart will find coming days of trial, shadow, and darkness.

And yet there is no reason to anticipate the day of ill and sorrow with dread and trembling. All things are under the dominion of the loving Jesus, and His word is, "*Fear none of those things which thou shalt suffer.*" Christ also suffered, leaving us an example that we should follow His steps. Though persecuted unto death, a man of sorrows and acquainted with grief, He soon lived again, and is alive and crowned for ever in heavenly majesty and glory. And as it was no loss to Him that He suffered, so neither will it be to those who like Him commit themselves unto God as unto a faithful Creator.

We may be disposed to pity the man who pines in sickness, or whose home bereavement has hung with desolation and mourning, or who is called to wrestle with the pangs and straits of poverty, or whom reverses of fortune have bereft of the accumulations of years of toil. But it is a misplaced pity, "for if ye be without chastisement, whereof all are partakers, then are ye bastards, and not sons." There is more of divine goodness and mercy in it than if it were not. When the burden is the heaviest, then redeeming grace is nearest.

There is nothing like the darkness to lift up people's eyes toward heaven. The afflictions of time, to those who love God, are all investments to yield the sublimer revenues in eternity. They are the opportunities God gives for the better exemplification and strengthening of our faith, and which open the way to immortal crowns. And shall we pity those to whom God thus comes with chance for grander promotions in heaven? Shall we deprecate what is sent to bring us to eternal glories? Nay, "Blessed is the man that endureth temptation: for when he is tried he shall receive the crown of life."

The great matter for us is to be faithful; that is, to be full of faith and confidence in the Lord

Jesus, and to be true to that faith even if it should cost us our lives. At the worst, the sufferings of time are limited and will soon be over. They endure but for a moment. They are light as compared with those which Jesus endured for us. And if courageously endured without faltering in our faith, they connect with everlasting gains. The cross is the way to the crown. Though our life here be a living death, if we but hold on victoriously in our sacred confidence the present dying will all the more certainly exempt from that worse death to come to the unfaithful and unbelieving. Christians have all their purgatory in this world, and beyond is "a crown of life" for every courageous and faithful soul. Yea, saith the Saviour, "Be thou faithful unto death, and I will give thee a crown of life."

There is yet one important remark thrown in parenthetically by the Saviour in describing the state of these afflicted Smyrniotes. Though their works were few and weak, their tribulation great, their poverty extreme, yet He says, "*but thou art rich.*" It seems like a contradiction, but there is a wealth which is poverty, and a poverty which is riches. The poorest to the world's eye may yet be the richest toward God, and the richest in the things of this world may be the poorest in the eyes of Christ. These people were rich in their poverty, and their very poverty was riches, just as the sorrows they experienced in this world helped to make clear their title to the priceless treasures of eternity. A believing poor man is ten thousand times richer than a Crœsus or a Rothschild without living faith and trust in Jesus. If we would be rich indeed, we must first of all have our hearts set on the true riches and live for the heavenly crown.

> Oh, give me the flowers that droop not nor die!
> A treasure up yonder! a home in the sky,
> Where beautiful things in their beauty still stay,
> **And where riches ne'er fly from the blessed away!**

Lecture Fifth.

Rev. 2 : 12, 13: "And to the angel of the church in Pergamos write: These things saith he which hath the sharp sword with two edges; I know thy works, and where thou dwellest, even where Satan's seat is: and thou holdest fast my name, and hast not denied my faith, even in those days wherein Antipas was my faithful martyr, who was slain among you, where Satan dwelleth."

THE Letter to the poor and sorely-tried church of Smyrna was one of almost unmingled eulogy and encouragement, even though it had false professors to contend with. Its afflictions seem to have been good for it, and to have helped to keep it alive and true to its Saviour and to its profession. It was different with the church at Pergamos. That was prosperous in some things, but defective in others. The Letter to it has in it various censures, admonitions, and rebukes. It had a distinguished and honorable record in some respects, but some things were creeping in which needed to be corrected in order to the maintenance of proper Christian fidelity and devotion.

The Saviour presents Himself to this church as "He which hath the sharp sword with two edges." In the preceding chapter this sword is spoken of as proceeding out of the Saviour's mouth. It is therefore something of a *word-sword*. The office of a sword is to pierce, cut, sever, and kill, and a similar office belongs to the divine word. Though intended to save, it is also intended to kill. Paul says "the word of God is quick and powerful"—a living and potent instrument—"sharper than any two-edged sword, piercing even to the dividing asunder of soul and spirit, and of the joints and marrow." It is not so much an instrument of physical death as an instrument of moral cleavage, which cuts into souls, penetrates consciences, divides between true and false, whether in doctrine, sentiment, or life, and acts as a killing thing to what is at variance with truth and righteousness. It makes havoc of the hopes and good opinions which sinners have of themselves, pierces, wounds, and lacerates their self-security, cuts right and left against everything contrary to God, hews down the towering conceit of the proud and self-sufficient, and utterly slays the false hopes by which many fondly deceive themselves. Paul at one time took great credit to himself as a holy and saintly man, and thought he was a very hero of Jehovah's cause while trying to crush out the growing Church of Christ. But when this sword of the Spirit penetrated his soul he says he "*died*." It killed him—killed him in that valuation of himself in which he previously lived and gloried. And there is always in the word an active judgment-power which slays the wicked, and under which the finally impenitent must go down into death eternal.

In this church of Pergamos there was a good deal which needed moral surgery. There was some moral cutting and killing to be done to bring all right—a severance between things which did not belong together, and the destruction of evils which had taken shape and were working unfavorably. Hence the Saviour addressed them as He who has the double-edged sword, intimating something of what He was about to say and do in the character He takes. The exhibition of the knife bespoke moral cleavage and dissection, in which there was to be no sparing of the wrong, and death to everything foreign and offensive to the truth. Nor is there any comfort, hope, or standing for any Church or for any man against the word and truth of God. There goeth forth out of the mouth of Christ a sword of double edge, tempered, like the old Damascus blade, to trim a feather and cut an iron bar, and fitted to pierce and cleave and smite and kill everything that rises against truth and righteousness. One reason why so many hate and avoid the truth of God is that it hurts them, awaking the lashes of conscience and utterly destroying their hopes. And this sort of hurt was now to come to this church.

But only favorable things are noted first. The same announcement made with regard to the other churches is made to this: "*I know thy works.*" These are sweet words to those who are honestly toiling in the Lord's cause, though anything but assuring to the unfaithful and the wicked. It surely is a comfort and encouragement to the good to know that every thought and act of devotion to the Saviour is like a ray of light rising to the approving view of Heaven, to be treasured among the glories of Jehovah's throne; that every deed of love and duty, however unknown to men, has a voice that is heard in heaven; and that though it should be no more than the gift of a cup of cold water to a thirsty disciple or a prayer of earnest intercession breathed in solitude, it is registered in the mind of Jesus for appropriate honor and reward.

But with our *works* Christ also notes our places and surroundings. The church of Pergamos was unfavorably located. It had hard struggles for its life because of its unfavorable neighborhood. But Jesus took account of this. The word is, "I know thy works, *and where thou dwellest, even where Satan's seat is.*" Whatever is to be understood by this throne of Satan, the language assigns to Pergamos the bad pre-eminence of being a head-centre of antagonism to Christ and the Gospel. It was a very unwholesome atmosphere in which to grow plants of grace, an ill vicinage for the development of a pure church of Christ. That little congregation was therefore like a bark launched upon a stormy sea—like a lone rose blooming amid desert sands—like a floweret amid Alpine snows—like a blossom opening out upon the bosom of an avalanche,—where existence was very precarious. But Jesus had not failed to note the fact, and to consider all the difficulties and perils of the situation.

Christians, especially young Christians, often find themselves in very unfavorable associations and surroundings. Sometimes they are thrown into godless families, where prayer is ridiculed, the Bible made a jest of, religion scorned, and anxiety about salvation rated as a craziness. Or their place may be in houses of business whose heads are mere worldlings or skeptics, and the employes are mostly profane and godless. Or they may be thrown into engagements, pursuits, and duties which for the time exclude them from the place of worship, from the Lord's Day rest, and from the company of fellow-believers. Or they may be forced along by a certain rush and tide of things contrary to their wishes and against their better convictions. All such are in adverse and trying situations, making it hard to maintain a correct and devoted life. But Jesus considers it, and knows where they dwell, and sympathizes tenderly with His tried and disabled children who fain would honor and serve Him better but for the hindrances they cannot control. He knows it to consider it, and to sympathize with the hard necessity, though not to excuse unfaithfulness. Because these people dwelt where Satan's throne was, they were judged with leniency; but wherein they were unfaithful or untrue they were still rebuked and condemned.

Barks on stormy seas, and roses amid desert sands, and flowerets amid Alpine snows, and blossoms opening on the bosom of the avalanche, may still live, and God means that they should live, and they blamably fail of their destiny if they do not. Good soldiers must do picket duty in isolation from the massed body of the army as well as stand shoulder to shoulder with their comrades in line of battle. We may not expect dahlias to flourish by the side of glaciers, but we may yet look there for plants and flowers, perhaps a little different in their order and less luxuriant and towering in their growth, but still holding up their little bells of sacred purity to God and reflecting from their ice-bound homes the rainbow tints and modest graces of the skies. And so it was in the case of this church of Pergamos. Though planted in close neighborhood with Satan's throne, it still grew some blessed flowers of grace and genuine devotion.

Notice the items mentioned to its credit:

"*Thou holdest fast My name.*" The Proverbs declare that "The name of the Lord is a strong tower; the righteous runneth into it and is set on high." And so Christians are said to be washed, justified, sanctified "*in the name* of the Lord Jesus." The name of Christ is that which presents Christ, which makes Him known to us, which brings Him within the range of our apprehension and faith. Holding fast His name is holding fast to *Him* as we have learned to know Him and to trust in Him.

There are many expressions and words by which Christ is presented to us and by which we learn who and what He is; but they are all His *name*. Confessing and holding to what we thus learn and know of Him as our Lord and Saviour is confessing and holding to His name. The angel said, "Call His name JESUS," which sets Him forth as *our Saviour*—the one in whom standeth our salvation. He was also "called *the Christ*," which presents Him as God's *anointed One*, the long-promised Prophet and King spoken of by all the ancient seers as He who was to come to be the deliverer of His people. Jeremiah said of Him, "This is His name whereby He shall be called, *The Lord our Righteousness;*" and Isaiah prophesied of Him, they "shall call His name *Imman-uel*," which, being interpreted, is *God with us*. All of these are alike Christ's name, and tell what He is, and express what we are to take and hold Him to be.

If He is our Righteousness, then He is the propitiation for our sins, taking them upon Himself to atone for and cancel them, while He puts His holy obedience and justifying merit upon us in their place. The whole doctrine of substitution, of redemption through His blood, of acceptance with God through the virtue of His sacrifice for us, is thus included. And to hold fast to this name of Christ is to believe in Him, to cling to Him as our substitute and propitiation, to plead and rest on His righteousness as the ground of our forgiveness and justification.

And as an indispensable prerequisite to His being our Righteousness His further name is *God with us*. No mere creature-righteousness could ever avail for us. Only He who is above law could merit by obedience to the law, and only in the nature which had sinned could the required obedience and sacrifice be rendered. He therefore had to be both God and man in one. Nor can we have a right and sure idea of God except as manifested in Jesus Christ. As we are sinful beings, we cannot know what to hope from God except as He has revealed Himself and His will in Jesus.

If He is just, how can He relax His justice to pardon sin? And if He is merciful to forgive sin and to require nothing for it, how can He maintain His moral government? How far, then, His justice will relax in the punishment of sin, or His mercy triumph in pardoning sin, no one can tell; and there is nothing certain on which to base our hopes. It is only as we see sovereign justice, a Father's love, and a Creator's power combined and harmonized in Jesus that we come to see and know how salvation can come. God cannot forgive sin without ample satisfaction for it; and yet He can forgive the greatest sinner because Christ has died and stands surety for him. Here alone we find a clear and certain basis for confidence and hope. Christ being the Lord our Righteousness, we see and know, to our joy, that God can be just and yet justify the ungodly. In nature God is above us, so that we cannot reach or know Him; in the law, He is against us and a consuming fire to the guilty, so that we dare not approach Him; but in Christ He is our reconciled Father, waiting and anxious to welcome us to His bosom.

And to Him we can now come with all the liberty and confidence of dear children.

This Name, then, this apprehension of the blessed Lord Jesus, these people *held fast*. There were some who would not at all believe or receive it, but these Christians held it fast. To their credit and honor it is said of them, "Thou holdest fast My name, and hast not denied My faith." Not all the terrors of martyrdom could induce them to let go their confidence and hope thus built upon the Saviour's name. They held firm, "even in those days wherein Antipas was His faithful martyr, who was slain among them, where Satan dwelt."

And this is ever the chief thing in Christianity, that we hold fast to Christ's name as the anointed Saviour, the Lord our Righteousness, God manifest in the flesh. Without this all knowledge, all works, all virtues are nothing toward our salvation, and can give us no sure hope of pardon for our sins—no ground on which to count on heaven. "*Dost thou believe on the Son of God?*" is ever the vital question with us; and without that faith there is nothing left but a fearful looking-for of judgment and fiery indignation. But, holding fast such a faith, and building only on this name of Jesus, we can afford to suffer for it in this world, and endure to be ridiculed, persecuted, and even killed; for He who is our Hope will not forsake us or go back from His name.

It is further particularly emphasized to the credit of these people of the church of Pergamos that they *had not denied the Christian faith;* in other words, that they were not ashamed of the Gospel of Christ. There was much in it by which they might have been tempted to be ashamed of it. Its Author was crucified as a malefactor and a slave. All the great and mighty of the earth despised it, and nobody of account paid any regard to it. Its professors were all poor, unlearned, and untitled people, held to be the dregs and offscourings of the earth. Some of its chief doctrines were considered absurd. Its principles were at war with the whole spirit of society as then constituted. It seemed to most to be nothing but a pestilential fanaticism which ought to be crushed out with the arm of power. It was a more unsavory thing to the élite of that day than Mormonism is now to the more respectable classes of our time. But still, they were not ashamed of it nor put out of countenance in holding to it and boldly professing it. And for this Christ commends them.

And with all that was humiliating in the Gospel, there was much more in which to glory. With the humiliation there was the constant presence of the divine. If Christ was born in poverty, in a stable, without earthly friends or favors, the angels of heaven filled the sky with joyous proclamations and highest songs over His nativity, and the stars pointed out that a glorious King had made His advent into our world. Never was there a march through human life so radiant from first to last with divine sublimity as His. Great Nature's powers were more at His command than Rome's legions at the command of Cæsar. The seas which rolled not back when Canute spoke answered to His orders and laid down their boisterous waves in tranquil quiet at His feet. Demons which no human power could dislodge quitted their hold and ran howling from His presence at His rebuke. Lepers, blind, deaf, maimed, halt, paralytics, and sufferers from all manner of disease took health and wholeness and renewed life from the virtue that went out from Him at His touch or His word. He needed only to speak to the dead and they lived · again. Though yielding Himself at the last to be shamefully crucified, all nature shook in sympathy with His death: the earth quaked, the rocks rent, the graves opened, the dead were startled back to life, and witnessing men smote their breasts and hasted from the scene in terror as if the day of judgment had come. And after He was dead and buried and sealed in the sepulchre, and a Roman guard set to watch His tomb, angels hovered inquiringly about the spot and friends and foes kept watchful eye upon it, and the universe waited in sabbatic pause while He lay in His grave; the time came when He started up again in resurrection power, bore away the gates of Hades, and He that was crucified came forth the everlasting Victor, the Prince of Life, the very Lord of glory!

And as to the Gospel itself, prophets foretold it;

the noblest poets of all time sung of its coming; the reigns of sublimest kings and the roll of special dispensations prefigured it; the holiest ceremonies from the foundation of the world typified it and pointed to it; the purest hearts and worthiest lives that ever graced the earth derived their inspiration from it; it was in the mind and foreordination of God ere the world was, and in view through all His providential dealings since Adam went weeping from Paradise. Though weak and despised, it was the only rising cause then on the earth, the most profoundly seated in the wants of man, and inevitably destined to grow and triumph till the Baptist's cry on Jordan's banks should be heard from the lips of nations: "Behold the Lamb of God, that taketh away the sin of the world." And what apostles claimed these people had occasion by experience to know, that it is "the wisdom of God and the power of God unto salvation to every one that believeth, to the Jew first, and also to the Greek."

There was therefore no reason to be ashamed of it, or to quail from holding firmly to it, in view of anything this world could bring to induce these people to disown it. Hence they held fast Christ's name, and did not deny the faith even when some of them had to die for it.

Antipas accepted death rather than give up or deny his Lord. Men might look upon him as a fool, a fanatic, a victim of delusion, a mad enthusiast, to throw away his life for his faith. The question might be, Why not use more moderation in his attachment to his creed? Why not yield a little and save himself from a martyr's death? But the name of Jesus was more precious to him than his life, and he preferred to be slain to a letting go of that name.

And do you suppose, dear friends, that he now regrets his choice? Can you think that he has been the loser for his faithfulness unto death? And why, then, should any of us let our profession droop and drag for the poor satisfaction of a little conformity to this corrupt and erring world?

It will not do to speak of being unfavorably situated. That can never excuse us. Antipas was a true disciple even where Satan had his throne. It will not do to say your business is so vexatious—your time so preoccupied—your friends so exacting of your attention—your duties so wearisome—your energies so tired out—your leisure so much needed for rest—your struggle for a livelihood so exhausting and severe—your acquaintances likely to think it strange for you to give attention to church and religion. God will not excuse because our circumstances are peculiar or unfavorable. Our trials may call forth Christ's sympathy, but they cannot justify unfaithfulness.

It is a great thing to have heard of Jesus and

to have learned His name, but it will be all the worse for us if we do not hold it fast. Whatever the trial, the word is, "If any man draw back, My soul shall have no pleasure in him." We have a Saviour and a great one, but we must hold fast His name and not deny His faith.

Lecture Sixth.

Rev. 2 : 14–16 : "But I have a few things against thee, because thou hast there them that hold the doctrine of Balaam, who taught Balak to cast a stumbling-block before the children of Israel, to eat things sacrificed unto idols, and to commit fornication. So hast thou also them that hold the doctrine of the Nicolaitans, which thing I hate. Repent; or else I will come unto thee quickly, and will fight against them with the sword of my mouth."

PERGAMOS was a city that rose to metropolitan dignity more than three centuries before Christ. It was founded in treachery by the treasurer of one of Alexander's generals, among whom his empire was divided after his death. This traitor carried thither great wealth and founded the dynasty of the rich Attalian kings, whose royal seat was Pergamos for nearly two hundred years. It was one of the wealthiest cities of its time, and famous for its magnificent library, which was second only to that of the Ptolemies in Alexandria.

Pergamos was situated in the midst of a very fertile valley, whose great productiveness naturally tended to develop a very sumptuous style of society. Its great wealth, luxury, and boasted learning, all arrayed on the side of a sensual and corrupting heathenism, perhaps more than anything else gave it the bad pre-eminence of being Satan's throne and seat. The historical descriptions of the place and people represent it as "epicurean in its philosophy and a nest of all sorts of gilded sensualities and conventionalized vices." It was the most intolerant toward the Christian teachings and testimony of any heathen city of its time; for while Christians were everywhere hated and despised, the first actual martyrdoms among the Gentiles seem to have occurred in Pergamos, where Antipas lost his life for his devotion to his faith. We know something of the style of life which characterized Pompeii; and Pergamos was even more corrupt.

In a place and condition of society in which Satan was pre-eminently enthroned it was hard for Christianity to get a firm footing, and those who embraced it were in great danger of becoming more or less infected and swayed by the general order of things with which they were in daily contact. Man is man, and he is very apt to take on much of the character of the society in which he lives, even against what he has been taught and has accepted as the right thing. Especially is this the case in a community of great wealth, polish, refinement, and celebrated for its cultivation and learning. We know something of what weak and ambitious people will do and sacrifice to get place and acknowledgment in what they call *society*—how prone many are to sycophancy and truckling to what they regard as the upper classes—how they will ape the ways and thinking of those who have a name for intelligence, taste, and high social importance. And it is not surprising that in a dominant pagan city like Pergamos, with its many rich and ancient families, recognized as a great university centre, and famed for the learning and culture of its population, many members of the Church should be seduced into damaging compromises with its sentiments, life, and fashions. So at least it turned out, as set forth in this Letter to the angel of the church at that place.

Having mentioned what was to the credit and praise of this church, the Saviour proceeds to note what was of a different character: "*But I have a few things against thee.*" The statement is gently expressed, for Jesus is full of tenderness to His people even when erring and at fault, but the language is stronger than that used toward the church at Ephesus. We are not to suppose our sins light because our Lord is tender. It is rather because the ailment is so serious that He approaches it so gently, as the object is to try to win the offenders back to proper life and spiritual faithfulness. He is not willing that any of His flock should perish, and the sicker the sheep He would recover the gentler is His dealing to save it. And especially where there is so much to approve and commend He uses every gentleness to heal what is wrong. But we dare not presume on that gentleness.

The first thing of which the Saviour speaks to the angel of this church is: "*Thou hast there them that hold the doctrine of Balaam*, who taught Balak to cast a stumbling-block before the children of Israel, to eat things sacrificed to idols, and to commit fornication." The minister is not charged with being of this party, and yet he is blamed that such people were tolerated in the church of which he had the oversight. He had not witnessed and striven against these errorists and corrupters as he should. He suffered them to remain in the church, notwithstanding their odious and unchristian sentiments. People of a bad life and a corrupted faith have no business in the Church, and those who have the oversight are to see to it that they reform from their ill ways or are thrown out from all church-fellowship and recognition. It may be a very unpleasant thing to do, but not to do it is to give countenance to sin and to connive at iniquity. Being grieved at it is not enough; there must be action—admonition first, and then, if there be no amendment, expulsion and excommunication. But the angel of this church, though pure and orthodox himself, was too lenient in his censures and dealings with certain members of his flock, and the Saviour makes it a matter of rebuke to him that he had there them that held to the doctrine of Balaam.

We are not to suppose that there were any who professed to be the followers of Balaam. Old errors revived generally try to get currency under new names. The people referred to called themselves Christians, and claimed to be very enlightened, liberal, and proper Christians. But they were really Balaamites. The principles which they entertained, taught, and put in practice as their idea of Christianity had in them the nature and essence of that sort of thing of which Balaam was the originator and exemplification. (See the accounts given in the twenty-second, twenty-third, twenty-fourth, and twenty-fifth chapters of the book of Numbers.)

Balaam was a prophet of God, and really spoke the word and truth of God. That point is not to be questioned. But he turned out to be a very bad man and came to a very sorry end. Prophecy is a gift and not a grace. There have been many instances in which God made revelations through instruments not at all partakers of His saving grace. Jesus tells of some who shall come up before Him in the judgment and say, "Lord, have we not prophesied in Thy name, and in Thy name done many wonderful works?" to whom He will answer, "Depart from Me, ye that work iniquity; for I never knew you." Balaam certainly did utter divine oracles, and claimed to hold himself bound faithfully to give what God said. He also had great fame as a sacred prophet. Hence King Balak sought his aid to put the curse of God upon the children of Israel and to prophesy evil upon them. It was a base desire, and Balaam was only too eager to serve him in his wickedness.

Balaam first tried legitimate ways, without avail, to obtain a divine expression adverse to Israel; but what he could not get by means of divine oracles he planned to accomplish by treachery, deceit, and the guiles of unprincipled women. If God's people could be seduced into apostasy and uncleanness, then God would be against them and Balak's wishes would be gratified; and this was now the devilish policy which he advised.

What moved Balaam in all this business was his eager desire to possess the honors and rewards which Balak held out to him. He "loved the wages of unrighteousness." With God's word in his mouth the devil's covetousness was in his heart. Balak approached him with presents, and offered him riches and honor. He proposed to take the prophet into his royal favor, enrich him with gold, and exalt him to the next highest place in the kingdom. And with these proposals the heart of Balaam was dazzled. He could not turn his back on such a splendid chance for wealth, standing, and worldly glory. He did not mean to let go his profession as a prophet. No; if Balak should give him his house full of gold he must keep strictly to the word God should put in his mouth. But if he could secure the proffered emolument without violating his conscience or compromising his principles, why not do it? And thus inflamed by his cupidity for Balak's treasures and favors, he made the effort and went on trying one thing and another until we find him at last advising the king to use the blandishments of women and lewdness to seduce the men of Israel and to beguile them to participation in the feasts and orgies of pagan worship.

This was Balaamism, and just what was reproduced in some of the members of this church at Pergamos. Though holding to Christianity, and in no way intending to renounce their profession and standing as members of the church, they would yet not be so bigoted as to wrong themselves out of much good fortune by refusing to concede anything to paganism. Why not be friends of these high people, yield a little here and there, and profit in temporal estate without letting go their Christianity? They would not be cynics. They could see no harm in accepting invitations to the entertainments of their heathen neighbors, in partaking of food and banquets on which the name of some heathen god was called, in visiting the pagan temples and shows on great occasions, in indulging themselves a little according to the customs of the community. This would please the heathen and secure their favor. What was a heathen god, at any rate? It was a nothing, a fiction—a thing which could neither help nor harm. Did they not know this full well? What fear that they should become infatuated worshippers of such nonentities? Could they not eat of idol meats and drink of idol drinks and sit at idol feasts and enter idol temples and be reverent at idol ceremonies, and enjoy some of the pleasures of idol frolics, without ever once lending their hearts to what they knew to be nothing but a fraud and a lie? What need was there for such rigid and bigoted scrupulosity when there was not the least danger of their ever turning heathen? And so they began to amalgamate with the rank and unchaste paganism which held dominion around them, and claimed it as their Christian liberty so to do.

Satan had tried them with violence and persecution, but, failing by that method, he plied them with social seductions, flattering them with worldly friendships, good standing with their heathen neighbors, credit for liberality, easy wealth, and gratifying pleasures. And with these lures they were drawn and enticed until it came to be a matter of doctrine and principle with them to make common cause with idolatry, holding it to be of no account one way or another, and maintaining that a Christian could still be a Christian even in heathen temples and while participating in heathen feasts. This was their Balaamism—their spiritual harlotry—which did so much mischief in the early Gentile churches.

The same is elsewhere spoken of. Peter speaks of some walking after the flesh in the lust of uncleanness, despising the dominion that would restrain them, presumptuous, self-willed, not afraid to speak evil of dignities and of things they did not understand, counting it pleasure to parade their scandals as those who riot in the daytime, sporting themselves with their own deceivings while claiming to take part in the feasts and sacraments of the Church, having eyes full of adultery, beguiling unstable souls, and having their hearts full of covetous practices after the manner of Balaam. He calls them wells without water, clouds carried by the wind, bombastic talkers, through lusts of the flesh and wantonness alluring good people into their abominations, promising them liberty while themselves the bond-slaves of corruption. Jude speaks of these same people as giving themselves over to the uncleanness of the heathen, filthy dreamers, railing at all spiritual authority, running greedily after the error of Balaam for reward, spots and scandals in the Christian feasts, trees twice dead, raging waves of the sea foaming out their own shame, wandering stars to whom is reserved the blackness of darkness for ever.

Nor is there another class of people against whom the Scriptures fulmine such terrible wrath and condemnation as those professed Christians who for worldly gain, pleasure, and carnal indulgence held it to be their right and privilege to join with the heathen and to do as they pleased on all these social questions. It was the particular fault and abomination of the times, which perverted, ruined, and destroyed more souls than all the persecutions of the pagan government. Nay, it is one of the particular ailments of the Church in all time, and especially again in our time, that many of its members, for their own ease, pleasure, and gain, claim it to be their right and liberty to join in the ways, habits, amusements, and society of the corrupt and idolatrous world while yet claiming to be very correct and orthodox Christians, if not Christians of a superior sort, quite freed from the bigoted and illiberal spirit of those who count such things an abomination. This joining of the worship of God with the worship of Mammon, this amalgamation of the children of God with the children of the devil, this bringing together of the table of the

Lord and the tables of demons, this holding to Jehovah and yet pleading for liberty to bow down in the temple of Rimmon, this gilding over of the service of greed, vanity, ambition, selfishness, carnal appetite, and sensual pleasure by a heart- less and skin-deep profession,—what is it but this selfsame detested Balaamism which leads to destruction, plague, and eternal death?

It was the bane and curse of the church of Pergamos that with all its faithfulness to the name and faith of Christ it had such people in it, and that they were allowed to remain in it without discipline and excommunication. And it is the bane and curse of the Church of our day to a still greater extent. I doubt if man has ever seen so many silver bridges between the Church and the world as modern Christianity has arranged and sanctioned to the weakening of itself and the ruin of souls. And few indeed are the professed Christians of our times who are not more or less tainted and swayed by the abominable "doctrine of Balaam, who taught Balak to cast a stumblingblock before the children of Israel, to eat things sacrificed to idols and to commit fornication."

And yet another detestable thing did the Saviour point out in this church at Pergamos: "*So hast thou also them that hold the doctrine of the Nicolaitans, which thing I hate.*"

In the church of Ephesus there is reference to

"the *deeds* of the Nicolaitans," which the members of that church hated and would not at all countenance. But what were only deeds and practices in Ephesus had grown to *doctrines* and principles in Pergamos, and what the angel of the church at Ephesus could not tolerate, the angel of the church at Pergamos allowed to have place and to put itself forth in teaching and dogma.

Our information concerning these Nicolaitans is not very complete, but the early Christian writers speak of them as a sect of the Gnostics, who held that the body is a corrupt thing destined to perish, and that it did not matter about what was done with it in the short time that it has to live. Hence they gave themselves free license in all sorts of corporeal impurities. Adultery, fornication, and every sort of fleshly indulgence they made no sin of, claiming that the death of the body would set the soul free from all condemnation. Not only plurality of wives, but community of wives, was part of their system. Eating things offered to idols and joining in pagan feasts and orgies were nothing wrong in their eyes. Nor did they hesitate to introduce heathen rites into Christian worship. In some of their characteristics they quite accorded with the Balaamites, but in others they were still more besotted and impure.

And to give some sort of dignity to their abominations these people claimed to have derived their practices and doctrines from the good deacon Nicolas, and so called themselves Nicolaitans, to the great scandal of a very worthy name. Their doings and principles were such that Christ declares He *hated* them.

Well also would it be for modern Christendom if it were less infected with this same spirit. But when we observe how lightly many regard the sacredness of marriage, the readiness with which its ties are dissolved, and the unconcealed libertinism and uncleannesses which even professed Christian people wink at and pass as trifling foibles, we are forced to the conclusion that the Nicolaitans have not yet died out.

Though men may connive at such things, the great Lord and Judge does not. If the pastors of the Church tolerate them without protest, and do not bring their authority to bear against the abettors of such unclean amalgamations, Jesus holds them responsible, and demands repentance and earnest purging out of the corrupting leaven on pain of His wrath. Such Balaamites and Nicolaitans must change their minds and return to a more consistent and thorough Christianity, or the sharp sword of double edge is drawn against them and they can only perish under it.

Dear friends, it is not possible to serve two masters. If we would hold fast the name and faith of Christ, we must let go the world and the following of its evil ways and uncleannesses, and abhor the very garment spotted by the flesh. "What fellowship hath righteousness with unrighteousness? and what communion hath light with darkness? What concord hath Christ with Belial? or what part hath he that believeth with an infidel? and what agreement hath the temple of God with idols?" "Ye cannot serve God and Mammon." One thing or the other we must be; and if not consistent, true, and faithful Christians, we are of the world and must perish with it. "Wherefore," the word is, "come out from among them, and be ye separate, saith the Lord, and touch not the unclean thing."

Lecture Seventh.

Rev. 2:17: "He that hath an ear, let him hear what the Spirit saith unto the churches: To him that overcometh will I give to eat of the hidden manna, and will give him a white stone, and in the stone a new name written, which no man knoweth, saving he that receiveth it."

WHAT Christ hates Christians must hate, or they incur the displeasure of their Lord. The angel of the church of Ephesus hated the deeds of the Nicolaitans, and was commended for it; the angel of the church of Pergamos was indifferent and tolerant toward these errorists, and he is censured for it, and required to repent of his faulty leniency or meet divine judgment on account of it.

It is sometimes thought that ministers are not to be fighting men, and that controversy is a great evil in the Church; but Christ here presents Himself as a fighter against evil and against the abettors of evil, and requires of His servants to do the same or accept blame and condemnation. Controversy, instead of being the bane of the Church, has many a time been its only salvation. What would have become of it in the time of Athanasius, or the time of Luther, had it not been for the tremendous controversy in those instances? To let things drift along as they will for the sake of avoiding sharp conflicts and disturbing collisions is to let the devil do as he pleases and to give over the precious things of God to disaster and ruin. The angel of the church at Pergamos acted on this principle, suppressed his indignation at the errorists who were ruining his church, and failed to withstand them that held the doctrine of Balaam and the doctrine of the Nicolaitans; and the Saviour faults him for it, and demands of him immediate repentance, on pain of coming against him with the sword of judgment. To refuse battle with errorists is to accept battle with God, and we can be at no loss to know what the issue must be. And the repentance required of the pastor at Pergamos implied that he was to make war upon these Balaamites and Nicolaitans, witness and testify with unflinching energy against their ruinous aberrations, recover them to truth and faithfulness if he could, otherwise to exclude them totally from the communion of the Church. Nor was there any other salvation in the case, either for that preacher or that congregation.

Balaam's aberrations brought him death by the sword of God's indignation. He perished with the king whose wickedness he was so ready to serve for a price, and with those who had become corrupted with his devices. The record says: "Balaam also, the son of Beor, they slew with the sword" (Num. 13:22). And so the threat here was that unless thorough amendment took place without delay, Christ would come quickly, and in like manner fight against these new Balaamites and Nicolaitans with the sword of His mouth.

And the execution of this threat would have touched not only those corrupt ones on whose account it was made. Such a judgment on the church would have affected the whole body. The sins and failings of unfaithful members implicate the whole Church. Judgments come by reason of the wicked only, but when they come the good have to suffer with the bad. As things are in this world, the gold and the dross are cast alike into the fire, though only the dross is to be consumed. When there is blessing on account of the good, the wicked share it; and when there is judgment for the wicked, the good and pious are made to feel it with the rest. Nor is it right that we should escape the tribulation if we have not honestly done what we could to remove the causes which have procured it. Communities are dealt with as communities, and churches as churches; and what happens to the body as such all the members together must share.

But while God thus judges churches and peoples in this world, this is not the final award to the individual members in it. The Church or State may fall and perish, but it does not follow that individuals belonging to it can have no better destiny. A Church may apostatize and come under the curse of God, and yet there may be in the midst of it some suffering individuals in no way responsible for the trouble, who stemmed the tide of evil as best they could, and held fast to the right in spite of it, faithful found among the faithless, to whom a better portion is reserved.

The individuality is still not sunk and lost in the community. There is another and further administration which dispenses to each one separately according to his works. And along with each of these addresses to the churches there is exhortation to individual members, and promise to each separate soul that overcometh, no matter what befalls the church as such. There have been saints under the worst apostasies and in the most evil times—jewels amid ashes, flowers amid deserts of barrenness. In the darkest days of the Roman Inquisition a martyr to his uncorrupted faith wrote on the wall of his dungeon: "Blessed Jesus, they may separate me from Thy Church, but they cannot separate me from Thee!" and many not written in the martyrologies of man are yet inscribed and canonized in the calendar of God because of their faith and faithfulness in the midst of the avalanches of apostasy and reigning sin.

The Gospel addresses itself to individuals: "*He* that hath an ear, let him hear what the Spirit saith unto the churches." Except as individuals hear and believe there can be no faith, no salvation. And hence also the promise is to each one separately: "To *him* that overcometh will I give to eat of the hidden manna, and I will give him a white stone, and in the stone a new name written, which no man knoweth saving he that receiveth it."

In each of these seven Letters the Saviour recurs to the description which contemplates Christians as conquerors, overcomers, persons who hold out in their faith and faithfulness to final victory. The figure implies conflict, hardship, adversity, antagonism, difficulty. A true Christian is a wrestler, a soldier, a combatant, who puts forth his energies to conquer, and who does conquer— if not at once, yet surely in the end. The whole current and spirit of things in this world, both within us and without, is contrary to faith and to a life of faith. The influences are strong to keep people from accepting and confessing Christ, and they are equally strong to pervert, corrupt, and hinder even after having taken hold of Christian life. The heart is deceitful, the world is seductive, and the devil is watchful and cunning; and all sorts of trials come by which honest souls are likely to be deluded, tripped up, diverted from the truth, betrayed into sin, and rendered untrue to their profession. And such is the situation in this world that we must conquer these evil influences or they will conquer us; and only he who does thus conquer is a true Christian.

In the case of these people of the church at Pergamos the more particular evils against which they had to struggle were the seductive influences of a rich, cultured, luxurious, and sensual heathenism, in which Satan had enthroned himself—compromises of Christian fidelity for worldly favor, patronage, gain, and pleasure; affiliations with the heathen in their feasts, banquets, and ceremonies; aping after the styles, fashions, and manners which prevailed in that corrupt and rotten community, and the justification of such abominations on the grounds of Christian liberty and right. It was no easy thing for those well-to-do to keep clear of these subtle and treacherous contaminations. Many prominent members made nothing of them, and still claimed to be as good Christians in their worldly conformities as any others. The minister was easy and reticent. The lures without were strong and attractive, and the example set by those of prominence in the chur.h favored this amalgamation of heathenism with Christianity and of Christianity with heathenism; and it required great moral courage, devotion, and uncompromising determination to stand out unflinchingly for the pure Gospel and a pure Christian life. It necessarily involved many an unpleasant collision and many a hard contest, both within and without, for those who would be Christians in deed, and not only in name, to be successful. Many a sore, trying, and disabling wound would necessarily be incurred, and nothing but hard fighting could give them the victory. But the Saviour was with them in their struggle to help them with His sympathies, word, and promises, and addressed a special promise to every one who should remain faithful and overcome in this heavy conflict.

There are several items in this promise. The first was, "*To him that overcometh will I give to eat of the hidden manna.*" The temptation which specially beset these Christians of Pergamos was, or earthly advantage, to partake of idol meats and heathen feasts, and so the promise is that if they would abstain from such improprieties, and hold themselves clean and separate from such contaminating feeding and carnal compromises, Christ would supply them with a far more precious bread. Rejecting the world's dainties for Christ and His pure service, He would give them "to eat of the hidden manna."

We know something of the miraculous food

with which God nourished and sustained His ancient people during their long and weary years of wandering in the waste and barren wilderness, and which the people called *manna*, "What is it?" for they did not know what it was. But it was a heavenly bread specially provided of God, which fell in little white flakes every morning for the day's supply, except on the Sabbath, to carry them through which a double portion fell on the morning preceding. And thus were the people fed during all their long pilgrimage until they came to eat of the fruits of the Promised Land.

That miraculous bread was the type of another and better bread for the feeding of souls and their nourishment unto eternal life. So the Saviour Himself has explained this in John 6, where He speaks of Himself as the true manna given of the Father from heaven: "The bread of God is He which cometh down from heaven, and giveth life unto the world. . . . I am the living bread which came down from heaven: if any man eat of this bread, he shall live for ever; and the bread that I will give is My flesh, which I will give for the life of the world. . . . He that eateth of this bread shall live for ever." This, then, is the true manna and food of souls in their pilgrimage to the better country, as the manna of the wilderness was the food for the bodies of the pilgrim tribes. This bread is given us in the Gospel to be received and fed on by faith in Christ as our salvation, and still more literally in the Holy Supper. By faith in the one, and by the same faith eating and drinking in the other, we are quickened and nourished unto life everlasting; and these Pergamites, as all Christians, by holding truly to the name and faith of Christ, were to have of this living manna for their perpetual nourishment and comfort as the help and attendant of their victory.

But this does not seem at all to exhaust the promise or to compass its more special meaning. When the tabernacle was built, command was given to take of the daily manna, put it into a golden pot, and lay it up before the Lord in the ark of the covenant in the Holy of Holies. Into that sacred place, the picture of the divine residence in heaven, no one but the high priest, and he only with great fear and trembling, dared to enter. A veil hung between it and the outer sanctuary which none but he could pass, and beyond which none but he could look. It was a hidden chamber in which there was a still more inviolable concealment of what was placed in the ark of the covenant. And the specimen of manna there preserved was the most intensely hidden. It was first of all closed in the golden pot, and the pot enclosed in the ark, and the ark enclosed in the unapproachable Holy of Holies. It was pre-eminently "*the hidden manna.*" And to this the reference here doubtless is.

This omer full of manna, thus laid up before the Lord and hidden from the view of men, was no longer corruptible, like that which fell daily around the camp, and which changed to putrefaction if kept over a day other than the Sabbath. It continued pure in its golden pot for generations. But if the manna which the people ate referred to the flesh of Christ given for the life of the world, this specimen of it, rendered incorruptible and laid up in the presence and dwelling-place of God, must needs refer to the same, but now in that condition of immortality and incorruption in which He ascended to the right hand of the Father.

We thus reach the sacred teaching that the heavenly food of true believers exists in two forms, though really of one and the same substance: the corruptible form in which it was given to death for the world's life, and the incorruptible form in which it now has place before God in heaven—the one of which we partake and on which we live in this our mortal pilgrimage, and the other hidden in heavenly glory where we can never see or approach it until this mortal puts on immortality and comes in true priestly character within the veil and enters whither the Forerunner is for us entered.

It is also very plain that the promise here, like the promises in the other of these Letters, refers to some benefit and favor pertaining to the future kingdom of glory, when this present life is over, rather than to something possessed and enjoyed in the present kingdom of grace. The Saviour does not say that He *has* given to Christian victors to eat of the hidden manna, but that He *will* do it in the future, which can only be when the warfare is ended and the victory is complete beyond any further peradventure. Every feature and implication of the case thus carries over to the immortal and heavenly state, when corruption has been swallowed up of life, for this hidden manna and for the eating of it which the overcomer is to have. Christ in glorified humanity is now hidden there. Flesh and blood cannot enter into that holy place, or eye of mortal look upon that golden pot of incorruptible bread which has thus been laid up in heaven. And the sweep of this glorious promise to the victorious Christian soldier looks to the life to come—to the immortal state—to admission into the veiled place of the divine residence—to likeness, fellowship, and beatific vision of the Redeemer in His heavenly glory—and to the impartation of His own glorious self to us as our immortal meat and drink and life and everlasting joy. Elsewhere in the Apocalypse we read that "the temple of God was opened in heaven, and there was *seen* in His temple the ark of His testament" (Rev. 11 : 19), and that after the seven last plagues are fulfilled men were able to enter into the temple, and so come to the hidden manna, then no longer hid from them, and, seeing it, to eat of it, and partake of its sublime incorruptibleness. And in this view it is questionable whether there is anywhere a sweeter and more precious personal promise than that which the Saviour here gives to the Christian victor.

But this is still not all. It is further added: *"And I will give him a white stone, and in the stone a new name written, which no man knoweth saving he that receiveth it."*

The blackballing the faithful one receives from the society of earth is to result in a happy election to the society in heaven. Having won in the conflict, there is given him the mark of honorable distinction—a token of free access to all the joys of the kingdom. So many interpretations of this promise run. But this does not seem to reach the special nature or the full meaning of the promise. The "*white stone*" is not a pebble used or cast by another, but a luminous and glittering jewel given into the victor's own possession, and in itself a sublime treasure to him. Entering into the holiest of all, he enters as an accepted priest, and he gets the most lustrous and precious sacred jewel of the priest. We can think of nothing but a diamond in the case—the Urim given to the high priest to be borne by him as a most sacred jewel, into which he looked with holiest reverence to see and read the responses and revelations of the Lord Almighty, and through which his soul came into communion with the mind of that Jehovah whose name was engraved upon it. *Urim* means *lights*, the lights and illuminations from Jehovah. And such a crystal gem of light, at once the token and the medium of the holiest communion with the Giver of it, the Christian overcomer is to receive.

And on this luminous gem there is to be a new name engraved—not the victor's name, but the Giver's name; and the newness of the name refers to some newness of character and of glory in Christ to be made known to and realized and enjoyed by the receiver of this gem which none but he can ever understand.

The immortal priest thus comes to partake of the immortal Christ as his life and food and joy, and receives the gem of immortal privilege, of divine illumination, and of insight into the mysteries and glories of Christ, which belong only to him that overcometh in the Christian conflict. As Phinehas was rewarded and honored with "an everlasting priesthood" for his zeal in vanquishing those sins to which the Old-Testament Balaam seduced Israel, so he who is zealous against, and effectually resists, the temptations and the sins of the New-Testament Balaamites is to be rewarded with the heavenly priesthood. The Ephesian overcomer is to eat of the tree of life which is in the midst of the paradise of God; and the Pergamite overcomer is to eat of the hidden manna, and possess the gem of heavenly lights and communings with the mind and character of Christ as His everlasting priest, with the freedom of all the mysteries of the Holy of Holies.

Dear friends, it doth not yet appear what we shall be. The light is too bright and dazzling for us to look into it or to penetrate its transcendent wonders. But it is the privilege of all to be the sons of God, sure of this, that when He shall appear we shall be like Him, for we shall see Him as He is. Meanwhile we have these earthly depravities, temptations, and lies to fight and overcome. We are soldiers, and the hardships of the long campaign and the weight of many a heavy battle are upon us. Often we may be sore oppressed. But our help is strong, our Captain is mighty, and the rewards of victory are worth ten thousand-fold more than all it costs. It is our business as our wisdom to fight on bravely, faint yet pursuing.

These Epistles are voices from the better land, full of melody and high promise to inspire us with energy and quicken our zeal. They come to us from Him who has been through the fight, and would bring us through to share with Him in the eternal triumph. And as we thus listen to the glorious things which the Spirit saith unto the Church, let us bind them as precious treasures on our hearts and hold on firmly to the name and faith of Jesus, knowing Who it is that has said, "To him that overcometh will I give to eat of the hidden manna, and I will give him a white stone, and in the stone a new name written, which no man knoweth saving he that receiveth it."

Lecture Eighth.

Rev. 2 : 18, 19: "And unto the angel of the church in Thyatira write: These things saith the Son of God, who hath his eyes like unto a flame of fire, and his feet are like fine brass: I know thy works, and charity, and service, and faith, and thy patience, and thy works; and the last to be more than the first."

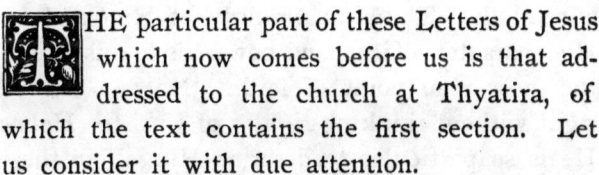HE particular part of these Letters of Jesus which now comes before us is that addressed to the church at Thyatira, of which the text contains the first section. Let us consider it with due attention.

You will remember that Thyatira was the place from which Lydia came of whom we read as the first disciple converted to the Lord on European soil. Paul found her with other women at the place of prayer by the river-side at Philippi, and spoke to them of Jesus; and the Lord opened her heart to attend to the things which he spoke. Whereupon she was baptized as a Christian, and afterward entertained Paul and Silas at her house. She was in Philippi selling purple goods for which Thyatira was famed. It may be that her permanent home was at Thyatira, and that on returning from Macedonia she may have been the first member of the church at Thyatira, as she had been of the church at Philippi. At any rate, there was a church at Thyatira in the latter days of the aged apostle John, and Lydia may have been among its members.

In the text we find two things to be noted:

I. *What Christ says of Himself;*
II. *What He says in commendation of this church.*

It is a great matter to know what to think of Christ and what estimate of Him to keep before our minds. To think wrongly of Him and of His character, offices, and powers is to mistake in the most vital point of faith. No one can be right without thinking rightly of Christ. Hence He is so particular to describe Himself in these several addresses. To the church of Ephesus He presented Himself as "He that holdeth the seven stars [ministers of the churches] in His right hand," and "who walketh in the midst of the seven golden candlesticks," which are the churches. To the church of Smyrna He presented Himself as "the First and the Last, which was dead, and is alive." To the church at Pergamos He presented Himself as "He which hath the sharp sword with two edges." And here He presents Himself as "the Son of God, who hath His eyes like unto a flame of fire and His feet like fine brass." The meaning is, that all He thus says of Himself to the several churches is everywhere and always true of Him, while the particular description in each specific case has special application to the state of things in the church addressed.

In this church of Thyatira there were some very wrong but very queenly assumptions which needed special rebuke and humiliation; and so the Saviour presents Himself here in His divine royalty as "*the Son of God.*" He would have all such pretenders and usurpers know and remember that He who speaks has the supreme authority and is the very Son of God Himself.

To the Jewish mind this designation meant participation in the divine nature and prerogatives, and presented a claim to be "equal with God." And so Christ here claims to be "the only-begotten Son of God," who came forth from the Father and is one with the Father. It was because of this claim that the Jews insisted on having Him crucified, holding that it was blasphemy in a man to make himself equal with God. But He still makes the same claim, and announces Himself from heaven as truly *the Son of God*. We therefore mistake our Lord if we fail to consider Him as God, very God of very God, and hence having supreme authority over His Church, from whose judgment there is no appeal, and against whose power no opposition can stand. No king's daughters and no authority or power of man can hold against the Son of God. His is no arm of flesh that the wicked may break it or that His people may trust in it in vain. He is true Lord and God, for He proclaims Himself "*the Son of God.*"

Many think that the reference is to the second Psalm, where we find the decree of the eternal Father, saying unto the Son, "Thou art My Son, this day have I begotten Thee. Ask of Me, and I shall give Thee the heathen for Thine inheritance, and the uttermost parts of the earth for Thy possession. Thou shalt break them with a rod of iron, Thou shalt dash them in pieces like a potter's vessel." The heathen may rage, and the people imagine a vain thing; the kings of the earth may set themselves, and the rulers take counsel together; but God hath set His King on the holy hill of His Zion, and to Him must all reverence be rendered, or we can only perish by the way. Men must hail Jesus as the almighty and everlasting Son of the Father or there is no hope for them. At His word the earth trembles; if He but touch the hills, they smoke; and when He shall lift the veil of dark clouds which now encompass Him, His enemies shall reel and stagger, and be swept away like stubble before the fire.

And with this presentation agree also the other particulars: "*He hath His eyes like unto a flame of fire.*" There is nothing more piercing than flaming fire. Everything yields and melts before it. It penetrates all things, consumes every opposition, sweeps down all obstructions, and presses its way with invincible power. And of this sort are the eyes of Jesus. They look through everything; they pierce through all masks and coverings; they search the remotest recesses; they behold the most hidden things of the soul; and there is no escape from them. As the Son of God He is omniscient as well as almighty. As Hagar in her grief exclaimed, "Thou God seest me," so the Son of God sees everything that is going on in His Church, and sees every one of us.

This is at once a very comforting and yet a very solemn truth. As far as we are honest, true-hearted, dutiful, and trying to be the disciples of Jesus, it is a glad thing to know that Jesus sees us and can read our thoughts and knows our hearts, and will do us justice. But when we think of our faults and failures and the many things which are not to our credit, it is a most impressive reflection that it is all "naked and open to the eyes of Him with whom we have to do." How solemn to think that the all-penetrating eye of the Son of God is upon each one of us now—in close contact with every heart here present—seeing just how we feel, with what ideas we came to this service, and how we are receiving these great truths!

We speak sometimes of secret thoughts, hidden feelings, things which lie buried in our souls from all human knowledge but our own. But there is no such thing in relation to Christ. He sees all and knows all. From Him there is nothing secret, nothing hid.

Many are not what they seem to be. What God made to express and show the soul is often trained to conceal it and to make an outward appearance of what has no reality within. The serene brow, the bright and candid look, the firm step, and the open countenance, meant to speak the innocence, truth, and moral dignity of the soul, are often imitated and feigned to hide from others the dastard spirit which reigns within. People often make a show of goodness and devotion, sometimes by self-deception, sometimes with deliberate intent, in order to gain favors or promote their own selfish ends. They use the refinements of life or the garb of piety to hide what God condemns and wishes to extirpate. Modern society is full of this elegant hypocrisy, and the people of the Church are not always free from it. It is one of the arts of our day to cover guilt with smiles, iniquity with fair-sounding words, and bad morals with attractive and fascinating manners. But Christ's piercing eye flames through all such falsities and deceits. People may impose upon each other and hide their real hearts from the gaze of man, but they cannot impose on Christ. He sees beneath all masks and detects the miserable lie. Even those latent propensities to evil which good people often feel, and those folded buds of covetousness, pride, ambition, impurity, or malice as they lie in the secret soul, and those schemes of evil which circumstances repress, those sympathies which we would fain conceal, those lurking passions which Providence keeps back from development, those secret sins and deeds of darkness which are so carefully shut in from observation, as well as the prayers and struggles of the conscientious,—Christ sees and knows, and has registered before Him.

And how dark must this earth appear to the bright, burning, and all-penetrating eye of Jesus, to whom all the hidden sins and falsities and corruptions of men are as naked and open as their more shameless vices! What a spectacle will the day of judgment reveal when all that is in people's hearts will be laid bare and every one is seen precisely as he is! There is, indeed, a covering for sin to those who will take it. God has covenanted to blot out the sins of them that embrace the great Propitiation; and His promise to such is that their sins and iniquities shall no more come into remembrance: "The blood of Jesus Christ cleanseth from all sin;" and where we have Jesus for our Advocate and Friend we shall never be ashamed. But His eye is very keen, and we cannot secure exemption by mere make-believes, shams, and halfway work.

But, further: "*His feet are as fine brass*"—"like unto fine brass as if they burned in a furnace."

Feet are the instruments of motion and downtreading. Brass tells of strong and imperious power for judicial administration. And fluent, glowing brass bespeaks intense and burning purity. Putting these ideas together, we have a vivid picture of the burning holiness and mighty strength of Christ to tread down whatever is opposed to Him, and to crush the unholy into everlasting fire.

Christ's eyes of flame to see all, and His penetration into all secrets, have a purpose. They are to enable Him to distinguish between the wheat and the chaff. And His feet of brass are for the treading down in judgment of all that is unholy and impure. As hypocrites and unbelievers are all known to Him, so He is armed to crush them in righteous indignation for their falsities and unfaith.

II. Notice now *what He finds in this church to commend.*

Farther on He tells of what was wrong; but with all the faultiness there was much good. In the very worst of these churches there still was something to approve.

It is a hard thing for a Church to become so totally apostate as to have nothing good in it. Amid all the depravity and corruption there still are likely to be some who really love and serve Christ. Sodom had a Lot; the bleakest desert has some green spots; the snowiest mountain still has some humble flowers; and so we may count that there are some good and believing people in very defective communions. And Jesus has eyes to spy them out, and a heart to honor and commend them if they are really to be found. He is not unjust to forget any one's labor of love, and is all the more sympathetic with His people because of the disadvantages under which they hold fast to Him. When Nathanael was hidden away under the fig tree communing with God in secret, Jesus observed him and noted his devotion; and the good works of His servants, though never made known to the world—those heart-prayers where there was no strength for more, those earnest desires to do which had to remain desires because there was no power to carry them into effect, and all that is attempted and achieved for God and righteousness—He sees and registers in His memory for blessing and reward.

There were believers in Thyatira in whose hearts dwelt the love and charity which true faith always works. They loved Christ, they loved His cause and His Church and His poor. And He here sent to them the comforting assurance that He knew it, and had taken due account of it to their credit.

It is a pleasant thing for any one to know and feel that his heart is right, and that he is doing what his conscience approves; but it is a still more precious thing to know that Jesus observes and approves it.

Very good service also had been done by some of these people of Thyatira. They not only loved, but they were active in ministries of love. Where they had opportunity they did good unto all men, especially to them who were of the household of faith.

There are many doors open for Christian usefulness. All can do something for the Saviour and His cause; and these had shown their devotion in such ways as were open to them. And this also the Saviour noted with commendation. Even the giving of a cup of cold water to a thirsty one in the name of a disciple has its record in heaven, and will be mentioned to our credit by our blessed Lord and Judge.

When Christ calls us to be Christians, He calls us to a service—to work in His vineyard, to lay out our talents for usefulness and profit—and it is a great matter to be found faithful, doing what we can, ministering according to our gifts. It pleases Christ and calls forth His commendation, and when we come to stand before Him in the day of reckoning He has told us that He will say to every such dutiful one, "Well done, good and faithful servant! enter thou into the joy of thy Lord."

But with this love and service there were also faith and patience. Moses endured as seeing Him who is invisible. This was living faith in God and the divine promises, and the root-principle which led him to choose suffering with the people of God rather than enjoy the pleasures of sin for a season. A similar faith and faithfulness existed in some of these Thyatirians. They had heard the Gospel, and embraced it, and turned their backs on the evil and idolatrous world to live for Christ and heaven. They had made their choice. They had given themselves to be the citizens of that invisible and spiritual kingdom of which Jesus is the Head. They had received the promises and embraced them, and confessed that they were strangers and pilgrims on the earth; and they were now on the way to a better country—that is, an heavenly. All this Christ assures them that He had noticed and had record of it in heaven.

There is nothing that more pleases our Saviour than that we should be full of faith and confidence in Him, His word, and His saving power. All that stands written in the Gospel He has caused to be written, that we might believe that He is the Christ, the Son of God, and that believing we might have life through His name. When on earth He departed from a certain country, and did not many mighty works there, because of the unbelief of the people. He loves to be trusted, and loves them that love Him, and stands pledged to bring to honor all them that put their trust in Him. And the great question which He asks of every one is, "Dost thou believe on the Son of God?" Everything depends on that.

And as service goes with love, so patience goes with faith—a readiness to endure and suffer for Christ's sake—a firm holding on in trial—a continuance in well-doing against whatever discouragements may come. And of this there were also some exemplary ones in the church of Thyatira. They had much to dishearten them. They were not only stigmatized and hated by their more numerous heathen neighbors, with all the common trials and temptations accompanying Christian life, but they had special conflicts and discouragements within the church itself. Their minister was an easy-going man, like Eli of old, quite too compliant in letting things have their way. In Ephesus there was much zeal for sound doctrine, and strictness in maintaining it; but here there was no discipline and no proper care on that subject. Not only were the most corrupting teachings allowed, but the most heretical and immoral pretensions and practices were permitted, if not encouraged. A large portion of the church was making common cause with heathenism, and promoting principles which overturned all Christian truth and morality. Another Jezebel had made her appearance there, doing as bad work for the church in Thyatira as Ahab's heathen wife had done for ancient Israel. An order of things had come about in which it was no longer an easy matter to be a true and faithful Christian. There was much to provoke and vex the souls of honest and virtuous believers. The cause of Christ was being so scandalized and perverted that there was strong temptation to abandon all connection with a fellowship embracing such corruptions and falsities. But they had patience and held on, unwilling to forsake the ship, though it had so many unclean and unworthy passengers aboard. And for this the Saviour commended them.

It was "through faith and patience" that the ancient Fathers inherited the promises, and we must ever let patience have its perfect work. It will not do to drop all and sulk away from place and duty because things do not go right or because some are mere hypocrites and unclean pretenders. The Church is Christ's, and we are not to forsake it because there are Jezebels in it who pervert its truth, belie its faith, and scandalize it by their bad lives. We cannot expect to have heaven on this corrupt earth. We will always have much to bear, and much wrong and vexation to put up with, and many annoying discouragements to meet, so long as this world lasts. Humanity is depraved and perverse, and its evils will manifest themselves in one way or another to disgust and grieve us. But we must not give up on that account. Christ had to endure great contradiction of sinners, and was even betrayed and denied by some of His own most trusted disciples; and His followers must expect disheartening trials of all sorts. He held on in His gracious work amid all His adversities, ever faithful to Him that appointed Him; and He would have us courageously follow His steps. We can never make things better by giving up to discouragements and trials. And, whatever the hardships may be, He takes notice of them, and His favor is with those who continue steadfast, "patient in tribulation" and slow to weary in well-doing. He takes notice of our patience as well as of our successful achievements, and our patient endurance is one of the things which He will honor and reward.

But there was still another commendable feature in the character of these Thyatirian saints. In spite of all their adversities, they were *grow-*

ing in their service of love and patience of faith. Their last works were more than the first.

People who act on mere worldly principles are apt to do their best first, and to count that that ought to suffice. If supplements are added, they are mostly feebler and done with less heart and diminished cheerfulness. Having done so and so, they are prone to think their part done, and that they are henceforth to be exempt. It was not so with these saints. They had done well at the beginning, and they were doing better at the last. And this the Saviour noted and commended.

It is meant that we should ever "grow in grace," in labors of love, and in the patience of faith. We are never done while we are in this world. If we have done commendably in the past, we are to try to do more commendably as strength increases and the circumstances call and require. Our Saviour expects this of us, and He is all the more pleased when our last works are more than the first. It is not meet that we should always remain babes in Christ, but that we should grow and progress in faith, knowledge, experience, patience, and all good works. Having been born into the kingdom, it is that we may develop into good, intelligent, active, and useful citizens in that kingdom. Having set our feet upon the way, it is that we may go on unto perfection. As children are always longing to be men and women, so we are ever to be aspiring to the full stature of men and women in Christ Jesus. And it is always more or less a reproach when for the time we ought to be teachers, and yet have need to be taught what are the first principles of the doctrine of Christ.

Dear friends, there is no standstill in living Christianity. If we have faith, it will work and grow by exercise. The moment patience, courage, and activity fail, Christian character stagnates and retrogrades. We must keep moving and doing, so that when the end comes we may look back upon lives fragrant with good deeds and holy services, and feel that we have at least honestly tried to do our duty and to fulfil our calling in Christ Jesus. And blessed is that disciple whose last works of love and service and faith and patience are more and better than the first.

Lecture Ninth.

Rev. 2 : 20 -23 : "Notwithstanding, I have a few things against thee, because thou sufferest that woman Jezebel, which calleth herself a prophetess, to teach and to seduce my servants to commit fornication, and to eat things sacrificed unto idols. And I gave her space to repent of her fornication, and she repented not. Behold, I will cast her into a bed, and them that commit adultery with her into great tribulation, except they repent of their deeds. And I will kill her children with death; and all the churches shall know that I am He which searcheth the reins and hearts: and I will give unto every one of you according to your works."

AFTER the exalted commendation of the laborious and increasing works of love and ministration, faith and patience, in this church of Thyatira, we would hardly anticipate much room for reproof and rebuke, still less for censures so sharp and threatening as those which now actually come before us. But the best of churches are often troubled with very unworthy members, and the worst are sometimes those who are most prominent, active, and pretentious.

Christ, however, is no respecter of persons. He is holy and true; His eyes are like a flame of fire; He searcheth the heart and trieth the reins; He sees through all pretences, disguises, and self-deceits; He tries activities according to their principles; He estimates people for what they are in reality; and He has feet of brass to bring fiery judgment upon men and women, high and low, who are found abusing and perverting their calling and profession, misleading His people and corrupting His laws and ordinances. His love is great, and His forbearance is not soon exhausted; but He is as holy, as loving, and as severely just as He is patiently forbearing. He has no compromises to make between good and evil, neither does He allow the one to be compensated for and offset by the other. Because people mean it well while yet greatly erring, or because they are looking to the more successful popularizing of the Church by doubtful proposals and impure compliances, they are not therefore excused and passed as unblamable. People must be right according to Christ, and not simply right according to their own judgments, notions, and fancies, or they set up a bar between the divine favor and themselves, and fall under rebuke and threatening instead of blessing and promise. And, comforting and assuring as were the praises which the Saviour here pronounced upon some, His accusations and condemnation of others were peculiarly sharp and severe.

It happened also that the centre of this particular plague-spot in the church of Thyatira was *a woman*. The Church has ever been much advantaged by the influence and activities of its women. They personally ministered to Christ in His arduous labors when on earth, and Paul has numerous special acknowledgments of the good services rendered to the cause of the Gospel by believing women. Women in general are more ready to take hold of sacred things than men. A right woman has more soul than a man, and has a more tender spiritual sensibility. Man was made first, and so was meant to stand foremost as the main outer wall of the great social fabric; woman was made afterward, to supplement what was wanting in man, to be a help to him, as the more graceful inner genius of adornment, moving with quicker and lighter step, speaking with a softer voice, taking hold with gentler and more persuasive touch, and encouraging, brightening, and mellowing with a more angelic love and service.

Christianity has honored and blessed woman as no other religion ever has done; and since the Redeemer of the world condescended to be born of a woman the sex has shown instinctive recognition of the blessing He has brought to them, and has never ceased to fill the prophecy of having been the last at His cross and the first at His sepulchre. It was not without significance for all time that the first person to whom the risen Saviour spoke was a woman, and that He gave to her a commission of love even to the chief of the disciples. And since that time women have ever been the most numerous class of His followers and among the most active and devoted of His saints, while woman's work in the Church has ever been of very great worth.

But the very qualities which prepare her for so much usefulness also render her capable of very much mischief. If the Church has been greatly blessed by the pious services of women, it has also at times been greatly harmed and hurt by the doings of women. Miriam long served Israel as a prophetess, yet from her jealous heart and evil tongue she stirred up a murmuring and revolt which carried with it even Aaron and the elders and produced a far-reaching trouble, which, but for the interposing judgment of God, would have involved the whole people in divine condemnation. And so the particular evil which troubled and spoiled the church at Thyatira was traceable to the activity of one of its prominent and influential women.

Her name was *Jezebel*, which means "the chaste," but she was in real character anything but what her name signified. Bearing the name of Ahab's queen, she shared largely in that noted woman's qualities, and her influence on the Thyatirian church was much like that of the ancient Jezebel on the kingdom of Israel. The ancient

Jezebel was the daughter of a royal priest of Baal, and was herself a patron and prophetess of Astarte and of the obscene orgies connected with the worship of that goddess. She also induced Ahab to recognize these abominations as part of the national religion. And so this Jezebel gave herself out as a leader of instruction and devotion, proclaimed herself a prophetess, and set on foot a system of things which swayed even the minister of the church, and found a large and influential following. She was doubtless a woman of genius and much force of character, and perhaps also of high birth and connections, to be able so to impose upon an otherwise good and faithful pastor and to mislead so many of his flock.

In the early days of Christianity it was common for the spirit of prophecy to be given to women as well as men, and for them at times to exercise their gift in the Church even as the men, though it soon became necessary to interpose some constraints, that the bounds of modesty and decorum might not be transcended, as in the case of the heathen pythonesses, who prophesied with dishevelled hair and raving extravagances, regardless of all decent propriety. "Philip the evangelist had four daughters, virgins, which did prophesy," and it is mentioned to their credit; and so it doubtless was in many other instances, according to the ancient promise: "Your sons and your daughters shall prophesy." One of these Christian female prophets this Jezebel claimed to be, and hence was given great "liberty of prophesying," so that she came to be regarded as an authority and gained great influence.

Nor does the Saviour say that she was not supernaturally impelled. The only point made in that regard is that her spirit was not at all the Spirit of God. She claimed that it was of God, and may have persuaded herself, as she persuaded others, that her inspiration was divine, but all the circumstances and facts of the case show that it was an inspiration from below and not from above. If she had the gift, she certainly had not the grace.

There was demoniac inspiration among the heathen, and there are many passages of Scripture to show that similar infernal inspirations manifested themselves among professing Christians. Paul and John both give rules for trying the spirits to test whether they are of God or not. Jesus Himself says that "many shall come in the day of judgment, saying unto Him, Have we not prophesied in Thy name, and in Thy name have done many wonderful works? unto whom He shall say, I never knew you; depart from Me, ye workers of iniquity." The false prophet of the last times is spoken of as doing great wonders, and deceiving the dwellers on the earth by means of the miracles which he has power to do. And from the days of Jannes and Jambres in Egypt satanic and demoniac powers and inspirations have run parallel with the manifestations of the Holy Ghost, often so cunningly disguised as to influence and captivate the confidence of men more than the true manifestations from God. Even to this day spiritists and mediums, men and women, are proud to say that they speak and do marvellous things by the inspiration and aid of spirits and powers from another world; and they have their followings too, as if they verily were divine oracles for the setting of this world right. That their inspiration is not of God their character and their teachings abundantly show; but that it is all sham and pretence I am not prepared to affirm. Only this I know: that their teachings are from beneath and that their whole system is in the devil's interest and service. There is no holy spirit in anything they say or do. And of this sort was the inspiration of this Jezebel, who by claiming divinity for her foul spewings overawed her pastor and led many of his flock astray.

The nature of her destructive heresy was of the same general sort as that which Balaam taught Balak for the ruin of Israel, and which Ahab's queen was so successful in introducing in the days of Elijah. The substance of it was the obliteration of the lines of demarcation between the

Church and the world, between Christian purity and heathen debauchery—the throwing of the sanctions of religion over carnal indulgence and impure life. The most shameless sins were practised and encouraged in the name of devotion as a triumph over Satan in his own dominions—a descending into "the depths of Satan," thereby to taunt and defy him. It was a devilish hallucination. It was Antinomianism of the worst and most vulgar sort. In the name of the higher Christianity it exalted Christian liberty to such a height as to make a virtue of defiant plunging into the basest crimes of heathenism to prove the sublime exemption which the Gospel works. To commit fornication, to live in impurity, to partake of the heathen feasts, and boldly to eat and drink what was dedicated to idol gods, as a matter of Christian freedom and in token of Christian triumph, was what they specially commended. Super-exalting the saying of Paul, that "there is now no condemnation to them that are in Christ Jesus," they completely set aside and nullified the further part of the declaration, that this exemption is only to those "who walk not after the flesh, but after the Spirit." They perverted the Christian calling so as to make it a call and license to uncleanness rather than to holiness.

We can hardly conceive how people could become so deluded and deceived; and yet such are the inspirations of spiritism even to the present day, to which so many commit their souls. Even some Christians seem to think it no great harm to indulge themselves after the world's ways and fashions, and that it is better for the Church to make free use of what the world likes and fancies. But a worldly Church and a fleshly and voluptuous life are ever at variance with Christ, who has only eyes of fire and feet of brass and words of condemnation for all such doings.

It would seem as if this were not the first time that special warning and reproof had been given to these false members of the church of Thyatira. The Saviour speaks of having given this Jezebel space to repent of her impurities. This implies that she had had due admonition concerning her evil ways. Perhaps the apostle John himself had been there administering his apostolic reproofs to these errorists. Some authoritative rebuke had certainly been given, even if the minister in charge had not done his duty in the case.

God is never summary in His judgments. "Sentence against an evil work is not executed speedily." He always gives timely warning before He strikes. His great desire is that sinners may come to repentance, and hence He is forbearing and long-suffering, warning them of their danger, signifying His mind, and giving them space to reform and better their ways. The crimes of the old world cried long to Heaven, while prophet after prophet was sent to rebuke them and call the erring ones to repentance. Even after it repented God that He had made man, and He had determined to destroy the rebels from the earth, He delayed one hundred and twenty years while Enoch and Noah preached to them of righteousness and a coming judgment. When the sins of the Canaanites came up before God and their extermination was announced, four hundred years did the judgment linger while Abraham, Lot, Isaac, and Jacob sojourned among them as God's witnesses to lead them to reform. He bore long with Ahab, and raised up Elijah to rebuke him and to give due warning to the infamous Jezebel of the fiery judgments that impended. And so it is the principle of His administrations to give due warning to offenders and time for them to repent before He allows judgment to strike.

But there is a point beyond which God's forbearance will not go, and then the visitation is all the more terrible if the wicked have failed to profit by His leniency and admonitions. He had given this Jezebel space to repent, "*but she repented not.*" She had only despised reproof and gone on with her wickedness, until now her probation was at an end. There was to be no more delay. Judgment was at hand, and terrible that judgment was to be.

There were several classes of offenders in this instance—some guiltier and more responsible than others, and so there was a graduation in the punishments.

First and guiltiest was this woman Jezebel, who claimed to be a prophetess and who was the inspiration and head of the debauching mischief. She had paramours whom she had drawn into her uncleanness. And the sentence was, I will cast her and them into a bed—not simply a bed of sickness or a bed of death, but that bed of which the Psalmist spoke when he said, "Though I make my bed in hell." "Into great tribulation" they were to be cast. And this sentence was now to go into effect unless the guilty parties should "at once repent of their evil deeds."

But this woman had children, perhaps natural children—at least children in the sense of disciples and followers of her pernicious teachings. These had been seduced, deceived, and imposed on, but still were not excused or exempted. Their sentence was to be killed, to suffer an evil death, to be suddenly cut off. And so marked was the judgment to be that all the churches should know how Christ searches the hearts and reins and rewardeth every one according to his works.

Dear friends, it is a fearful thing to be indulging our own lusts and pleasures and to be deluding ourselves with the Christian profession and hopes while we consent to run with the wicked world and suffer ourselves to be contaminated with its impurities and sins. Come out from among them and be ye separate, saith the Lord. "Adultery, fornication, uncleanness, lasciviousness, idolatry, witchcraft, hatred, variance, emulations, wrath, strife, seditions, heresies, envyings, murders, drunkenness, revellings, and such like," are all works of the flesh and "depths of Satan," which no man can yield to and yet retain his Christian character and hopes. It is for these things that the wrath of God cometh upon the children of disobedience, and they which do them must thoroughly repent out of their evil ways or they can by no means inherit the kingdom of God. The flowers that spring from a true Christian heart are of quite another sort. "The fruit of the Spirit is love, joy, peace, long-suffering, gentleness, goodness, faith, meekness, temperance: against such there is no law; and they that are Christ's have crucified the flesh with its passions and lusts."

But for the rest that were in Thyatira, the better class of professors, those who had not been seduced into the infamous doctrines and deeds of this Jezebel and her lovers, those who had not known "the depths of Satan" as these heretics boasted of knowing, there was also a special word. It was a happy thing for them that they had not gone into this satanic school, that they had not lent themselves to experiment with what was lauded as the higher mysteries of Christian liberty. It was a good thing that they had been content with the simple knowledge of virtuous life and experience, without trying to know more by knowing evil also. But it was nevertheless a burden to them to keep up a perpetual protest and fight against these mischievous teachings and abominations.

It is a great misfortune when leaders and active members of the Church are not the right sort of people—corrupt in principle and life and not to be trusted. It makes it hard for those who are right, true, virtuous, and desirous to fill out the proprieties of Christian life and devotion. It is a great drawback and hindrance. It gives a bad name to the Church, so that one is half ashamed to belong to it, and some take it as sufficient excuse for staying out or staying away altogether. It often becomes a serious burden.

But Christ does not fail to sympathize with those who have to bear it. He requires of us to bear it—not to run away from it, not to become indifferent on account of it, not to drop out of our places and our duty for the filthy Jezebels who may be leading so many by the nose—but to stand firm and do our part with courage and fidelity. Jesus said to these better Thyatirian Christians, "*I will put upon you none other burden.*" This means that one burden at least *was* put upon them which it was their Christian duty to bear, and do the best they could under it until God's judgment should be executed and their relief come. And the bearing of this burden was that they were to resist the temptation to float with the muddy current of things about them, and cheerfully and unflinchingly to endure whatever inconvenience, sneers, or harsh judgments might fall upon them for their non-approval of what was wrong, and their refusal to run with the erring into the same excesses and impurities.

The truth is, that faithful Christians always have burdens to bear—burdens which sometimes become very heavy and disheartening. If they are not of one kind, they are of another. But we are not to give up on account of them. The nets are always breaking and the ships are always sinking, but as long as Jesus is aboard we will never go down. We will get to shore some time, and not without an enriching reward for our patience and fidelity.

There is often much to dishearten us in our efforts, to weary us in our well-doing, and to make us feel as if there were hardly any use in this perpetual fight with the indifference, the ill temper, and the lack or perversion of Christian spirit on the part of many with whom our lot is cast. But we must not give way on that account. Our duty is to hope on and pray on and work on. Christ is with us in the struggle. He knows what hardships and discouragements are upon us. He sympathizes with us, and while struggling with one burden He will not allow others to come, and will not permit us to be tried beyond what we are able to bear. The Jezebels and false ones will not prevail perpetually. The great Lord has His searching eye upon them, and His judgment will reach them in due time if they repent not. We cannot improve things by becoming unfaithful ourselves. And hence the words of the Psalmist: "Fret not thyself because of evil-doers, neither be thou envious against the workers of iniquity; for they shall soon be cut down like the grass, and wither as the green herb. Trust in the Lord, and do good, so shalt thou dwell in the land, and verily thou shalt be fed. Delight thyself also in the Lord, and He shall give thee the desires of thine heart. . . . I have seen the wicked in great power, and spreading himself like a green bay tree; yet he passed away, and, lo, he was not: yea, I sought him, but he could not be found. Mark the perfect man, and behold the upright; for the end of that man is peace"

Lecture Tenth.

Rev. 2 : 25-29: "But that which ye have already, hold fast till I come. And he that overcometh, and keepeth my works unto the end, to him will I give power over the nations: (and he shall rule them with a rod of iron; as the vessels of a potter shall they be broken to shivers:) even as I received of my Father. And I will give him the morning-star. He that hath an ear, let him hear what the Spirit saith unto the churches."

THE Saviour is still addressing the few faithful Christians in Thyatira. It is plain, however, that the words are meant for the whole Church of all time. It is not possible that power to rule the whole world and dash nations to pieces, and the possession of the morning star should pertain exclusively to these few Christians in that one ill-conditioned church. Besides, there is here an admonition to hold fast *till Christ comes.* This seems quite incongruous as a direction to a congregation that the Lord knew would become extinct long ages before His coming, though very suitable as addressed to the whole Church, whose business it is to keep itself in continual waiting from age to age until He does come. And so also the concluding admonition designates what is here addressed to the

Thyatirians as addressed "to *the churches*"—not to the few people of one church alone, but to the universal Church of all time. So we are likewise driven to conclude, since every one that has ears to hear is admonished to give attention to it. These words are therefore to be regarded as the Saviour's words *to us* as well as to these Thyatirians.

The passage consists of two leading sections, with the second coming of Christ as the point of separation between them. The first section relates to time this side of the second advent, and the second section relates to time beyond the second advent. The one gives a chapter of things to be accomplished in the present earthly life, and the other gives a chapter of promises to be fulfilled in the period following Christ's return.

Notice, then—

I. *The requirements respecting this world.*

This faithful remnant in Thyatira had done exceedingly well for their circumstances. Their activity, their charity, their services, their fidelity, their patience, their endurance, and their keeping of themselves from the base debaucheries of knowing "the depths of Satan," were favorably noticed by the Saviour, and His sympathies were with them in the burdens that were upon them. So far, so good. But matters were not to end here. Probation was not yet over, and they were to see to their after-life with the same devotion and diligence which they had given in the days preceding. We are never done working, watching, praying, and achieving as long as we are in this world.

1. They were to hold fast what they had. They had the word and ordinances of God. And these are very great things to have. These made them Christians, and gave them their hopes, and had brought them to the activities, affections, and attainments which commended them to Christ's favorable regard.

We sometimes forget how much we owe to the Bible and those Christian institutes and teachings which have made our lot so blessedly different from that of the heathen. It is a great thing to have the Gospel ever sounding in our ears; to have ministers to teach it; to have Christian influences around us to condition our homes, temper our laws, and influence the habits and character of the community in which we live; to have the means of grace by which to come into fellowship and communion with our Saviour and our good Father in heaven; to have a throne of grace to go to in our wants, troubles, and trials, and a blessed heaven to look for as we are compelled to lay us down to die. These are not matters of course. They are what we have received from the Gospel which our fathers have handed down to us. But for the good providence and grace of God in bringing them to us, and causing us to believe in Jesus and His word, we would not have them to bless and comfort us in our earthly pilgrimage as they do. Nor is there anything on earth that could compensate for the loss of them. To hold them fast, and to find our chief treasure and consolation in them, are ever our highest privilege and Christian duty. Hence the word to these Thyatirian Christians to hold fast what they had.

To let go of the Gospel is to let go of everything. To become indifferent to the word and sacraments of Christ is to let all the great things of our salvation go by default. We must be faithful in our adherence to them and in our endeavors to transmit them in their purity to the generations that come after us, even until Christ Himself shall come.

2. These people were to maintain the conflict unto victory. Christian life is a perpetual war and strife with the evil that is in us, with the sins that beset us, with the influences and temptations of the world around us, with the errors that abound in the Church and all about us, and with the ills and trials of this life. Satan is ever active in all these things, and we are in constant danger of losing our faith and of being drawn aside from the paths of righteousness. Therefore

we have to be always on the alert, and ever stirring ourselves up afresh to the utmost fidelity and effort, that we may not be overcome of evil and come off conquerors in the end. Heavy as the warfare may be, we must keep it up; never suffer our interest or our energies to flag, nor think of giving up the fight until the final victory is won. For only unto them that overcome, being faithful to the end, is the promise given.

These people had a hard time of it to maintain their Christian character. They were in the midst of a world of enthroned heathenism and corruption. The church to which they belonged was full of false teachings and debauching error. All the tendencies of society were adverse to faith and purity. But this was not to discourage them. They were to be all the more inflexible and determined because their situation was unfavorable, and to fight the harder because the enemy was so strong. Victory would come if only they pressed on to it with proper courage and vigor. And to this they were to give and keep themselves, with their eyes constantly on the goal that was held out to them.

3. Furthermore, they were to keep Christ's works unto the end. Christ's works are the true Christian works over against the false ways and wicked doings of Jezebel and those who fall into her snares and seductive devices and teachings.

The works of these heretics were works of the flesh and works of the devil—works contrary to Christ and His teachings. Christ's works are the works of the Spirit—devotion to the faith, love, purity, and the deeds of charity—keeping to that "wisdom which is from above, which is first pure, then peaceable, gentle, easy to be entreated, full of mercy and good fruits, without partiality and without hypocrisy." Having embraced Christ as the foundation of their confidence and hope, they were to build up upon it the structure of a good and active life—not wood, hay, and stubble, which could not endure the test of judgment, but gold, silver, and precious stones—that they might have praise and gain when they came to answer in the final account. No mere works, however good and excellent, can ever avail to save us unless they be built on Christ as the great Foundation; but, built on Him and in obedience to His word, He accepts them as His works, and if persevered in to the end they bring to us great recompense of reward. Hence all the sublime honors promised to these people were conditioned on their keeping of Christ's works and their faithful continuance in them unto the end.

These three things, then, constitute the great calling and duty of Christians in this life. What we have in and through Christ by faith in Him we must hold fast till He comes. The conflict with depravity and sin we must maintain unto final victory. And the works of Christ we must keep unto the end. To this we are called by the Gospel, and by this means alone can we come to the possession of the glorious things which are here held out to the faithful.

And to this we have ample incentives. The hardships, strife, and struggle will not continue always. The grand promise is that the Saviour will soon come again and make an utter end of this mixture of good and evil and this constant turmoil and conflict between the two. If we should die before that time, it will make no difference. We will then rest from our labors, and the resurrection will find us the same as if still living at the time. That coming is the great crowning-point and consummation of our destiny. Whether it should be in our lifetime or not till long after we have passed away from the cares and activities of this present world, on that the Saviour would have us keep our eye fixed, and to live and look and wait for it as the time when He proposes to terminate all our disabilities and to fulfil to His faithful people all His grand promises. Here we have only duties, trials, hopes; but when that point in the divine administrations is reached, then hope will become fruition, and eternal rewards will take the place of conflicts and toils. Quite another order of things shall then be introduced, and quite another state of affairs will come into play.

Notice, then—

II. *The promises respecting that world to come.*

Our toiling, striving, and working in this world are not to be in vain. There is full compensation for them soon to be realized. Our best endeavors here may seem to be wasted. Very little gain or fruit may we see from them. We may often be tempted to drop our hands and say, "It is no use." Our best efforts may sometimes appear as just so much thrown away. But it is not so. The word of our Saviour has put in an effectual bar against all such feelings and thoughts. He knows how prone we are to become desponding, discouraged, and faint, and therefore He has put before us the grandest assurances that heart can conceive.

1. First of all, our salvation will be secure. By fulfilling the inculcations laid upon us we will share the victory and triumph of Christ Himself. As He bore our sins in His own body on the tree, and there received upon Himself the full penalty due to them, they shall no more hold against us. Cancelled in His blood, they are done away, blotted out, exscinded for ever. His death and resurrection, sealed to us in our baptism, is a receipt in full against them. All judgment for them is past, and we stand justified as

though they had never been. Having conquered death and come out from under it in the powers of an endless life, death is no longer any harm to us. It can only end our labors, aches, and sorrows here, while beyond are resurrection and life more exalted and glorious than if death had never been. Because our Saviour died for us, and is alive as the Lord and Master of death and hell, we shall live also, undamaged by their power. In a word, we shall be *saved*, all dangers past, all troubles over, all disabilities of our fallen condition reversed and gone. This in itself would be quite enough to compensate for all the costs and efforts of a godly life. But, great and transcendent as it is, it is only the substratum and lower plane of what is held out to the faithful child of God.

2. A sublime office and authority will be conferred: "He that overcometh, and keepeth My works unto the end, to him will I give power over the nations; and he shall rule [shepherdize] them with a sceptre of iron; as the vessels of a potter shall they be broken to shivers, even as I received from My Father."

What a promise is this! Who could ever have thought of such a thing as that the poor, despised, and suffering children of God should rise to the dignity and glory of invincible lords over all the nations of the earth? Nay, with the words of

Christ here and elsewhere so clear and positive before us, how few Christians rise to anything of even a faint conception of the transcendent promise! But they are Christ's words, and they mean what they say, and they are unmistakably true.

Look at the presentations on this point: "Do ye not know that the saints shall judge the world?" Does not the Psalmist tell of a coming morning, even the morning of the resurrection, when "the upright shall have dominion over the dwellers in the earth"? Does he not tell, again and again, of a time when it shall be the high honor of all God's saints to wield the sword of double edge, to execute vengeance on the heathen and punishments on the people, to bind their kings with chains and their nobles with fetters of iron—to execute upon them the judgment written? (Ps. 149: 5–9). Is it not declared in Daniel that the saints of the Most High shall take the kingdom, and that the kingdom and dominion, and the greatness of the kingdom under the whole heaven, shall be given to the people of the saints of the Most High, whose kingdom is an everlasting kingdom, and all dominions shall serve and obey Him? (Dan. 7: 18, 27). Did not the Saviour say to Peter that "in the regeneration, when the Son of man shall sit in the throne of His glory," they which have followed Him shall sit upon thrones of judgment?

(Matt. 19 : 28). In John's visions of what is hereafter to come to pass has he not told us of a multitudinous Man-child whom the dragon sought to devour, caught up unto God and His throne to rule [shepherdize] the nations with a rod of iron? (Rev. 12 : 5). Did he not see thrones, and God's faithful ones who share in the first resurrection seated upon them, and reigning with Christ as His king-priests, very "kings of the earth," who bring their glory and honor into the heavenly Jerusalem, in the light of which the saved nations then living are to walk? (Rev. 20: 4–6; 21 : 24–26)? And what does all this mean but exactly what the Saviour tells us in the text?

Dear friends, I am sure that the Church does not half see or believe the transcendent things which God has arranged and decreed concerning them that love Him and do His commandments. We talk of being *saved*—if only we are *saved*—while Jesus is talking of lordships, princedoms, regencies, and eternal authority and dominion.

The promise now under consideration connects directly with the second Psalm. We are there told of the decree and appointment of the eternal Father constituting His only-begotten Son the absolute King and Sovereign of the world, whom the kings of the earth and its rulers shall withstand and resist, but whom He will one day rebuke and vex and break with a sceptre of iron, dashing the rebellious to pieces like a vessel of pottery, and subjecting the nations unto Himself as His inheritance and possession. It is to this the Saviour here alludes in speaking of what He has received of His Father. And in the execution of these His judgment administrations, and the subjugation of the nations by His invincible power to His rule and government, He here engages to give His victorious people a part and share, *even as He has received from His Father*.

It is a mistake to suppose that the earth is to be annihilated and cease to be, or that it is ever to be denuded of its population. God made it to be inhabited, and placed man upon it to multiply, replenish, and subdue it. Hence we read of generations and generations world without end. "The end of the world" that we hear of is not the end of *the earth* or the end of generations on the earth, but only the end of the present order of things on the earth, the end of the present age and fashion of the world, the turning of man's day into the day of the Lord, and of man's mortal rule into the immortal dominion of Christ and His saints. That change comes when Christ comes again, when He will gather His people, whether dead or alive, to be with Him and to share in the work of judging the wicked world and forcibly reducing the rebellious nations into subjection to their rightful Sovereign, even to Christ. And this judging, shepherdizing, and subduing of the nations by an invincible rule or sceptre which must break and destroy all who resist it, is here the subject of the Saviour's promise to the victors who now keep His works unto the end. Nor is this all.

3. The further promise here is to him that overcometh and keėpeth Christ's works unto the end: *"And I will give him the morning star."*

But what new and strange proposal have we here? What means this morning star? Great kings and mighty rulers are called stars, and so are prophets and ministers of the Church; but this is a peculiar star and of pre-eminent brilliancy and distinction—the star that leads the heavenly hosts, shines on when others have faded away, heralds the dawn, and ushers in the day—*the morning star.* And we have only to look a little farther on in this book to find an authoritative declaration as to the identity of this star. Jesus there says, "I am the Root and Offspring of David, and the bright and morning Star" (chap. 22 : 16).

This star, then, is Christ Himself, but Christ in a particular stage and department of His grand redemptive work—Christ as the Herald and Inbringer of the day of final glory—Christ in the attitude, office, and administrations of the ending of this night of time and the ushering in of the fulness of His triumph and kingdom.

Christ gives Himself to His people now. He is their chief treasure as their Sin-bearer, their Teacher, their Forerunner, their Advocate with the Father, and their present and ever-sympathizing Friend—the Captain of our salvation; but then He engages to give Himself to them as something transcendently more, even as the forthcoming Sovereign of the world, the Breaker of Satan's rule, the Destroyer of Antichrist, the omnipotent Subjugator of the nations to His dominion.

It is night now, but there is a morning coming—the morning of resurrection, the morning preceding the noon of final glory, the morning when deliverance is to come to the Church and the upright enter upon dominion. And the Star of that morning, as of all other blessed mornings, is Jesus. He is its light, its glory, its joy, the Herald and Bringer of all that makes it glad. As Balaam saw Him from afar, He then shall appear as the Star out of Jacob, armed with a sceptre to smite the four corners of Moab and to destroy all the children of the wicked one, even as the King higher than Agag, stronger than the aurochs, and invincible as the devouring lion. As He Himself has said, "Then shall the Son of man sit in the throne of His glory, and before Him shall be gathered all nations"—"When He shall come to be glorified in His saints, and to be admired in all them that believe." And Himself, as He then shall come forth in His imperial majesty, does He here promise to give to every victor who keeps His works unto the end.

Wonderful promise! Behold the crowned elders on their golden seats round about the throne flashing with the symbols of the divine majesty, and the living ones six-winged and full of eyes conjoined with the throne and sharing in its awfulness of glory—all as seen in the vision of John, and you have these blessed victors in the possession of "the morning star." Our hearts tremble at the blaze of glory, dignity, authority, and power which shines forth in the description. And to have it in blessed fruition as our own is what the Saviour here promises when He says to every finally victorious Christian, "*and I will give him the morning star.*"

Said I not right, dear friends, that our Christian toiling, striving, and working in this ill world are not in vain? Is there not in the realization of all this an overwhelming ampleness of recompense for all that our devotion and fidelity may cost us during these few fleeting years? What more could we ask or think than is here pledged to us by our blessed Lord if we but keep His works unto the end? With such prospects ahead in the near future, and Christ's own word as our security for their attainment, and His resurrection as their indubitable seal, what is there in all the discipline, duties, hardships, discouragements, and adversities attending a life of faithfulness to God to be for one moment considered over against such a recompense of reward? Well might we be called on to rejoice and be exceeding glad amid reviling and persecution and all the ills that can befall us for our Christian faith; for great indeed is our reward in heaven.

Let us, then, be stirred up by these precious words of our Saviour to hold fast His truth and our profession, to keep diligently to our places and our duties as His called and chosen ones, to bear willingly whatever burdens His providence may lay upon us in this world, to endure hardship as good soldiers of the cross, and to set ourselves with unflagging constancy to keep His works unto the end, that we may come off more than conquerors through Him who loves us and washed us from our sins in His own blood and engages to make us kings and priests unto God.

And if any one hath an ear to hear, let him not fail to hear, and take earnestly home to his soul, what the Spirit saith unto the churches.

Lecture Eleventh.

Rev. 3: 1-3: "And unto the angel of the church in Sardis write: These things saith he that hath the seven Spirits of God, and the seven stars: I know thy works, that thou hast a name that thou livest, and art dead. Be watchful, and strengthen the things which remain, that are ready to die: for I have not found thy works perfect before God. Remember, therefore, how thou hast received and heard, and hold fast, and repent. If, therefore, thou shalt not watch, I will come on thee as a thief, and thou shalt not know what hour I will come upon thee."

THE city of Sardis was once among the noblest of the East. Its situation and its climate were exceptionally fine. It had excellent mountains and was washed by a river famous for its golden sands. It was the capital city of the kingdom over which Crœsus reigned, whose name has been the symbol of riches ever since his time. It had a temple as renowned as that of Ephesus, and far more ancient. It had a palace of gorgeous magnificence. It was a centre of wise men as well as rich men, and numbered Thales, Cleobulus, and Solon among its inhabitants. Full in sight were the gigantic *tumuli* of the Lydian monarchs, and around them spread the plains where Xerxes massed his mammoth forces when he went forth for the subjugation of Greece. And scarce was there another spot on earth with which more varied and more vivid remembrances are associated.

But, though connecting with a number of the greatest names in history, and a place of great importance under various empires for almost two thousand years, successive sieges, sudden surprises, earthquakes, and conflgrations, and the changing vicissitudes in earthly affairs have long since reduced it to a perfect desolation, with nothing left but a few paltry huts, the fanes of dead religions, the tombs of forgotten monarchs, and a few scattered ruins, with the wild trees growing in the banquet-halls of its former kings. And as it went with Sardis, so has it gone with the church of that city.

By whose ministry or by what special providence this church was founded we are nowhere told. The ruins of a Christian edifice have been identified as the church of St. John, and he perhaps was the man who first planted Christianity there. The only name historically associated with the church of Sardis is that of Melito, who was its bishop about the middle of the second century. But there is everything to beget the belief that it was a church of distinguished prominence. The character of the place, the wealth of the people, and the fact noted by the

Saviour that it had a name to live warrant the conclusion that it was regarded as a model church and one in high esteem by the other churches in Asia Minor. Whatever its inner character may have been, it had a name and fame at least in its outer manifestations of Christian life, enterprise, and strength. And to this church the Saviour now comes to give His estimate and judgment, both for its learning and for ours as well.

1. *Notice in what attitude He presents Himself.*

"These things saith He that hath the seven spirits of God and the seven stars."

A very important and very delightful truth here comes to our contemplation. Whatever the need of the Church may be, there is everything in Christ to meet the want. He has "*the seven spirits of God*"—that is, all the plenitude and ampleness of the Holy Ghost—for the illumination, quickening, sanctification, and abundant help of all His people. If they are in darkness, He has the fulness of the Spirit to enlighten them. If their life is feeble, their faith weak, their devotion cold, He is possessed of the power and grace to revive them and bring them to new spiritual vigor. And, whatever their infirmities may be, they have only to look and apply to Him and the requisite help is at hand. For He has "the seven spirits of God."

Men have debated whether the Holy Spirit proceeds only from the Father, or, as we confess, "from the Father *and the Son*." Christ's own word as here spoken should settle that question. "The seven Spirits of God" are the plenary and manifold fulness of the Holy Ghost; and, as Jesus claims to have these, and has them to impart, He must be God, and the Holy Ghost issues from Him the same as from the Father. Certainly we have in Him all power and grace to help in every time of need.

Great and manifold are the offices of the Holy Ghost. He is called the *Paraclete;* and a paraclete is an instructor, witness, monitor, helper, guide, and comforter. The giving of the Holy Ghost is an endowment with power from on high —the gift of a divine presence to quicken, energize, establish, equip, lead, and prosper in all sacred experiences and activities. There is nothing that we more need, or that the Church more needs to keep it alive in faith and good works, to give it efficiency, consolation, spirituality, and joy, than such a Paraclete. But for all these offices Jesus has and sends the Holy Ghost, and gives Him to all them that ask Him and submit themselves to His word; for He is able to save them to the uttermost who come unto God through Him.

Furthermore, with the seven spirits of God He has also "*the seven stars.*" "The seven stars are the ministers of the seven churches." This means that He has instituted the ministry, that He calls men into it that He owns them and their ministrations as part of the holy organism by which He dispenses life and salvation. They are His ambassadors. By them He speaks. Dealing with them in their holy office is dealing with Jesus. They have no right to go beyond His word or to do in His name what He has not commanded. They are His; He owns them and provides them for His Church, and He holds them to strict account for the manner in which they discharge the duties of their high office. No minister is in any respect independent of Christ, and no church is independent of the ministry Christ has constituted for its service. If a church has a good and faithful minister, Christ has sent him and made him what he is, and will never cease to qualify and send faithful ministers into His churches if people will look to Him for them and profit as they should by the ministrations of those whom He sends.

And it is also a great and comforting truth that Jesus has these stars, equips them for their places, sends them to serve His flock, holds and controls them for the supply of His Church's needs. Hence also He charges all His people to pray the Lord of the harvest to send forth laborers into His harvest. They are also worth praying for, for how shall men hear without a preacher? and how shall they

TO THE CHURCH OF SARDIS. 181

preach except they be sent? A good and faithful minister is indeed a star in Christ's right hand—a light-bearer and light-giver to the children of men.

Thus, then, as the possessor of all the powers of the Holy Ghost, and of the ministry appointed for the Church, Jesus here speaks to the church in Sardis.

2. *Notice what He finds in this church.*

Nothing was hid from Him. He needed not that any one should tell or testify as to the state of things. His eye searches the hearts of all His people. He knows their works and all that pertains to their condition. He understands every one of us through and through—all that we are, all that we do, all that we think, and everything concerning us. And His judgments are infallible.

He saw in this church in Sardis that it had a name, a good reputation, and was credited with a great deal of activity and life. Perhaps it had much wealth. Perhaps it was very liberal in its contributions for the general cause. At any rate, it had a name for being a live church. No fault is found with its orthodoxy. It is not censured as giving place to false teachers or harboring false and unworthy members. It seems to have been orderly, peaceful, respectable, and outwardly influential. And if everything had corresponded with its reputation and the outward appearances, it would have been perhaps the completest and most honorable of the seven.

But things are not always what they seem or deserving of the credit which they receive. While this church had a name for life, it was really to a great extent dead. It was actually dying. It had a reputation for life, while it was largely *dead* as to true spirituality. There was a reputable form of godliness, but it did not have the proper power. There was plenty of gentility and an honorable external estate, but there was much inward stagnation, worldly contamination, and spiritual decay. There were a few who had not defiled their garments, but the majority partook of the character imputed to the people of Sardis in general. There were works and activities, but they were much soiled and not filled out toward God. There was a weakening in the power of faith. Death was creeping over the souls of the people. A process of dying had set in, which had taken possession of many and was extending more and more, demanding a prompt and vigorous reformation to prevent things from becoming like the valley of dry bones in Ezekiel's vision.

It is hard to conceive of a more unfortunate condition for a church than to have a name to live while virtually dead. It is not so bad to be dead and to know it, wearing no disguise and without hypocritical show, as to have the ghastly skeleton clothed with a feigned life. To be dead, with the mere semblance of vitality, is more disgusting than to be laid out in undisguised death. It is a sad thing to contemplate the bare possibility of such an estate as having a name for life and yet being dead. But such, alas! is only too often the case with churches and with people who profess to be Christians. Even as human eyes see, instances of the kind are not wanting, and we have reason to suspect that there are many more quite veiled from human sight who to the all-seeing eye of Jesus are really but walking sepulchres in which there is only deadness and decay.

Nor should we too confidently turn away from the description as not possibly applying even to ourselves. There may be orthodoxy, and yet spiritual death. There may be a reputation for living devotion and godliness, and the true life of the Spirit of God be absent from the soul. There is such a thing as impressing others, and even ourselves, with the idea that we are all right when the hand of death may be upon our whole spiritual nature. A corpse can be galvanized into the motions and mimicries of life while yet it is as dead as a stone. And we all need to try ourselves well, lest, having a name to live, we should yet be dead.

3. *Notice what Christ demanded of this people.*

Very tender and gracious is our Saviour, even to the weakest and unworthiest of His flock. Wherein they are not right He is anxious to bring them right, and so orders His providence and word that they may become sensible of their faulty condition and have the opportunity and means of recovery before things have gone beyond remedy. We know how reluctant He was to give up the rebellious people of Israel, and what tears and lamentations He gave out over Jerusalem when He saw that the day of grace was past and all further hope was gone. With what touching pathos have those words thrilled down the centuries from the side of Olivet!—"O Jerusalem! Jerusalem! thou that killest the prophets, and stonest them that are sent unto thee! How often would I have gathered thy children together, as a hen gathereth her brood under her wings; but ye would not!" And with still more tenderness is He moved toward those of His own flock whom He finds out of the way and ready to perish. Therefore, with the utmost gravity, and yet with the most affectionate tenderness, He here appeals to these failing Sardians and to all in like condition to revive and save them, and admonishes them of what alone can do away with the trouble.

First of all, He calls upon them to get their eyes open, to become wakeful, to stir themselves up to watchfulness. The import of the expression is precisely that of Paul to the Ephesians, where he says: "Awake, thou that sleepest, and arise from the dead, and Christ shall give thee light."

It appears that these people had rocked themselves to sleep in their faith. They had become so self-satisfied that all anxieties were allowed to slumber. It was a sleep that meant death if not aroused from it; but it was not yet so deep that there was no more hope. And what they were now to do was to stir themselves up to more wakefulness, more vigor, more spiritual earnestness. They were not out of danger, but they were not alive to it. They had become inert and drowsy in religious duty, but had no right consciousness of their situation. They were gradually sinking into a state of death, but had no serious concern about it. This state of things was now to be broken up, their anxieties quickened, their flagging energies aroused. They were to trim afresh the lamps of their profession, and to set themselves on the lookout for the perils that impended over them.

Furthermore, they were to strengthen what remained and was ready to die. Not everything was yet dead. Their profession still continued. Some works were still being attended to, but with a spirit so indifferent, heartless, and perfunctory as to be more dead than alive and fast tending to extinction. Everything needed tonic and revival. And to this they were now to give themselves.

When people become lax and complaining with reference to the Church, and religious duties become irksome, and interest and spirit in sacred things become dull and secondary, it is high time for them to bestir themselves, turn over a new leaf, and strive for a new baptism of the Spirit, that what is thus lame and weak may be healed and strengthened, lest everything of their Christian character should die out. Backsliders must return, take hold afresh, set out with new vigor, and stir up the gift of God that is in them, or all their religion must pass for nothing. What has been done scantily, imperfectly, intermittingly, if not grudgingly, must be entered upon with a new heart, higher resolve, and more earnest devotion, or everything must fail.

And in order to this these people were to recur to their first experience, and call to mind how it was with them at the beginning. They were to remember how they had received and heard; with what self-sacrifice and holy unction the apostles had preached to them and labored among them in order to bring them to faith in Christ; with what glad devotion they had grasped hold of the word of promise that was thus brought to them; how different were their feelings, zeal, and earnestness then from what they had now become; and by honest repentance and fast-clinging to what they then so eagerly received get themselves back again to the same devout and hopeful condition.

It is a good thing for Christians betimes to remember how it was with them when they first set out to be the servants and children of God—what a lively perception of duty, and tenderness of conscience, and sincerity of endeavor, and completeness of surrender to Christ, and fulness of determination then marked them—that they may see in how far they have sunk away from their first love, and thus move themselves to do their first works over again and strengthen what is ready to die. The first in all these churches was the best, and so it is apt to be with Christians in general. And hence the Saviour's words are always in place, calling upon us to remember how we received and heard at the beginning, and set ourselves to hold fast and repent, and get ourselves back again to our first love.

4. *Glance for a moment at the consideration by which the Saviour enforces and impresses these demands.*

Man is a reasoning being, and capable of being moved by rational motives. Jesus does not command as a tyrant. He asks and enjoins only what is reasonable and what addresses itself to our consciences and judgment as proper and right. We find ourselves in a certain condition and compassed about by a certain order which is fixed beyond our control. We are moral beings, and cannot escape moral responsibility. We are here passing through a period of probation with a view to very exalted promotions and honors. There is a time coming when this probationary scene must end and the results of our faithfulness or failure be reached. And, as Christ has come and opened up to us a blessed immortality, and called us by the Gospel to keep ourselves in preparation and readiness for the revelation of His glorious kingdom, so He has promised to come again to receive all His faithful ones to Himself. When that coming is to be He has nowhere told us and no man knoweth. We only know that it is to be, that it will be a time of transcendent blessedness to those whom it finds ready and waiting for it, and that for the careless, indifferent, and unready it will be very calamitous, cutting them off from the honors of the kingdom, consigning them to the trials and sufferings of the great tribulation which shall befall the wicked world, and making their salvation "so as by fire," if, indeed, they are ever saved at all. And this mysterious, eventful, and impending coming again of the Lord Jesus is what He here puts before these drowsy and dying Sardians to tone them up to life and duty.

What if the great day should be suddenly precipitated upon them in the condition in which they then were? What if the view of the judgment-throne should break upon them with no better preparation for it than having a name to live and yet being so deep in spiritual death? What could they expect in that case but to be "left," being accounted unworthy to escape those things then coming on the earth or to stand before the Son of man? Of what high and glowing honors would they thus have failed for ever! But just these deplorable calamities does the Saviour put before these dull, slumbering, and dying saints as the grand moving reason why they should at once wake up, shake off their deadness, and put themselves in earnest duty and honest waiting and watching for their Lord. "If therefore thou shalt not become awake and watchful, I will come on thee as a thief, and thou shalt not know at what hour I shall come upon thee." That is to say, all sleepy and unwatchful people shall be taken by surprise; the decisive hour will come upon them unawares, and the result shall be the loss of those dignities and honors to which all hearers of the Gospel are now called.

Nor is there anything in the Scriptures more constantly used by the Holy Ghost or better fitted to stir up sleepy Christians to their duty, or to tone up decaying piety, than this doctrine of the coming again of Christ and the need to be looking and watching for it every day, that we may be found of Him in peace, and not suffer the sore excision which must then befall the unready. Again and again the solemn command is to keep awake and watch, since we know neither the day nor the hour when the Son of man cometh. Whether for the warning of the wicked, the encouragement of the saints, or the stirring up of the hearts of ministers and people to scrupulous fidelity to duty, the word continually is, *The Lord is at hand*—Behold He cometh—The time is come that judgment must begin—Blessed is he that watcheth and keepeth his garments. And one reason why the Christianity of our day is so flabby, so lacking in life and earnestness, so ready to make common cause with the world and its vanities, is that the great doctrine of the near and impending coming again of Christ has so much dropped out of the thinking, preaching, belief, and understanding of the Church. Did people but remember and realize the momentous truth that any day or night the trump of judgment may be sounded and all present opportunities be suddenly cut short, a very different state of things would exist and life would instantly take the place of death. Oh, that the Church might awake to the momentous things that must shortly come to pass!

And what guarantee have we, dear friends, that

any moment may not be our last? Who can tell how long he has to live or how quickly the trumpet of judgment may sound, the dead be raised, and all God's ready saints be changed and caught away in the twinkling of an eye? Luther gave it as his belief that it would be about Easter-time that the Lord would come; and what if it should be the Easter of this present year? I dare not say that this is the time, neither dare I say that it is not; for no man knoweth or can know. But it is just as likely to be in such a year as this has so far been as in any other. And our Saviour would have us lay to heart and consider how it would be with us if He should now come.

Let us, then, not trifle with the momentous possibility, but heed the admonition from our Lord to get ourselves awake to duty, to strengthen the things that remain, to repair what is wanting, and to set ourselves right, lest He should come upon us in the stealth and unexpectedness of the thief, and all should be disaster before we know it.

Lecture Twelfth.

Rev. 3 : 4-6: "Thou hast a few names even in Sardis which have not defiled their garments; and they shall walk with me in white: for they are worthy. He that overcometh, the same shall be clothed in white raiment; and I will not blot out his name out of the book of life, but I will confess his name before my Father, and before his angels. He that hath an ear, let him hear what the Spirit saith unto the churches."

IT is very seldom that a church becomes so corrupt as to have no genuine Christians in it. As there is no visible church in Christendom in which all the members can be counted as saints, so there is scarcely a confessed church which has no good and faithful children of God in it. There was an Enoch and a Noah in the midst of the dreadful apostasy which brought on the Flood, a Job among the emirs of Arabia, an Abraham among the idolatrous population of Ur, a Lot even in Sodom. And so in the midst of the deadness of the church in Sardis there were some happy exceptions, some scattered lights amid the darkness—like Savonarola, Wickliffe, Huss, and Luther amid the abounding gloom of the ages preceding the great Reformation.

We must not conclude too unfavorably where things look ill. The stars are not all gone because the sky is overcast. Amid the dreary snows and ice-rivers of the Alps and the Apennines there still may be found here and there a solitary flower. We search in vain for a wilderness so sterile as not to have in it some spring, some oasis, some tree or shrub or blossom. When Ahab had destroyed the prophets of the Lord, and Elijah thought that he alone survived, faithful among the faithless, God's eye still noticed seven thousand who had not bowed the knee to Baal. And in the days of Malachi, when almost the entire nation had become apostate, there still was a remnant that feared the Lord, who spake often one to another, and whom God had entered in His book of remembrance as His in the day that He should make up His jewels.

It is wrong to assume that there is nothing in Christianity, or that religion is a sham, because there are so many faithless people in the Church; so much empty profession; so many betrayals of confidence; so much deceit, uncharity, and baptized guilt; so much cloaked and gilded ungodliness; so much boastfulness of life where there is so much death. Sad as the facts may be, God has not left Himself without witnesses. There are some names "even in Sardis which have not defiled their garments"—some good men and true in whom the cause of Christ is justified, its saving virtue proven, and its glory demonstrated—men in whom its life still is preserved and perpetuated, who stand as monuments to the faith, the lights of their country, and the salt of the earth. If it were not so all would go to utter desolation. Hence Sodom's judgment lingers while Lot is within its gates. Till Christians have escaped the doomed city of Jerusalem stands invulnerable. Great Babylon itself is secure until God's people have come out of her. And the fact that things still go on in the Church and in the world as well as they do proves that true faith and genuine godliness have not utterly disappeared, and that there are still some genuine saints with garments undefiled.

I. *Note the Saviour's description of these people.*

He says of them that they "have not defiled their garments." A man's clothing is that which is next to him—that in which he puts himself forth—that in which he lives, moves, and acts. And so there is another sort of clothing which does not come from the weaver's loom and is not fitted by the tailor's hand. It is what we have around us in the world, the facts and circumstances of our life-contact with the earth and the things of the earth, our relations and associations. Every one thus has his vestment. No one in this respect is naked or divinely intended to be.

Christianity is not a divestiture of one's self of domestic and social surroundings. It is not the stripping off of the proper garments in which alone a man can properly live. Seclusion, solitude, asceticism, monkery, and cloister-life, severed from all connection with the ordinary world, is a species of denudation and nakedness outside of the divine order. All natural surroundings and honest pursuits, with all the cares, anxieties, toils, and even sorrows, which they bring, are for our greater comfort, usefulness, and glory. He who cuts himself off from them cuts himself off from God's natural sacraments. They are our proper clothing, to warm, protect, beautify, and bless us. They tend to ennoble, not degrade. They have a spiritual aim, and a spiritual value also, if they be rightly managed. Our business as Christians is not to cast them off, but to wear them, live and act in them, only so as to keep them without being draggled and defiled.

The atmosphere of this world may be unfavorable to purity. There is a constant tendency to taint. Silver will tarnish unless pains be taken to keep it clean and bright; and so our surroundings are liable to corrosion and soil if we be not on our guard. Even the best vestments are liable to take on filth, contagion, impurity, and disease. There can be no putting forth of life on earth but it is exposed to uncleanness. In society, in business, in the home, and even in the church, there is constant liability to slovenliness and defilement. James charges against certain Christian professors that their garments were moth-eaten, and the Saviour Himself speaks of the necessity of watching and keeping our garments.

It therefore belongs to true Christianity not to try to get away from ordinary life, but to live and act in such a way as to keep our garments clean. Washed and made white in the blood of the Lamb, they can also be kept white and clean even in the midst of all the dust and filth of this unclean world. If the Church, as such, is dead and corrupt, there is no reason why we as individuals should be. If others wallow in uncleanness and glory in their shame, there is no occasion for us to follow their ways. Joseph could pass through trial to princely honor, and maintain himself from first to last, without becoming unfaithful to God and righteousness. Daniel could maintain his purity unimpeachable through dynasty after dynasty in Babylon's unholy court. And as the blessed Master was in the world without being of it, using it as not abusing it, so may we also, in our degree, make our passage through it in contact with its sins without contracting its impurities.

Absolute purity, except in the merit and righteousness of Christ, we cannot have on earth. Weaknesses, errors, and infirmities cleave to us all our lives through. We cannot travel without dust. The rust will settle on the purest metal. But we need not keep the dust on us nor suffer the rust to eat the metal up. These people in Sardis managed to have clean garments, though in contact with very great corruption and decay. They maintained themselves in living faith and purity where everything was full of defilement and deadness. With their robes washed and made white in the blood of the Lamb they wore them without soil. They had turned from dumb idols to serve the living God and to wait for His Son from heaven; and in this service and waiting they continued. If the name or profession of others was a lie, it was not a lie in their case. They may have had a hard struggle for it, but they continued faithful. If others were lured by the siren songs of worldly compliance, they were not. If others were content with a name to live while spiritually dead, this could not be said of them. Alive to the truth and to their Christian calling, they continued steadfast in the same. They had "not defiled their garments."

II. *Note the Saviour's commendation to these faithful ones.*

Though hidden away in a congregation so dead, He had not overlooked them. Jesus sees and notes the humblest and most hidden of His saints, and no matter how bad, diseased, or decayed may be the church to which they belong, He knows them and takes due account of them, and has them credited in His memory and affection.

These were perhaps the least popular and the least influential of all the members of the church in Sardis. If they spoke out, it is plain that but little regard was paid to them. Perhaps they were credited with being religious over-much—with being too scrupulous, too fanatical, too strict, and more disagreeable than pious. Perhaps they were put aside, blamed with insubordination, censured as disturbers and trouble-makers, because they protested against the worldliness and deadness which had taken possession of that church. But Christ here speaks for them, vindicates them, declares them "worthy," and gives it as their lot to walk with Him in white.

The most neglected and despised on earth are often the most esteemed in heaven. It matters not for the standing of men in the eyes of this world or in the eyes of a dead and dying Christendom, provided they have the life of saints as well as the name—the power of godliness as well as its form. They are not unknown to Jesus. His favor is on them in all their trials. They have status in heaven which the highest in this world's esteem might well covet. And they have an Advocate and a blessed record on high.

"It is very beautiful to observe the gracious

manner in which the Lord recognizes and sets His seal of allowance to the good which he anywhere finds. Abraham said 'that be far from Thee to slay the righteous with the wicked;' and it is far from Him even to seem to include the righteous and the wicked in a common blame. He who delivered Noah from the destruction of the old world, who drew just Lot out of Sodom, who could single out from the whole wicked family of Jeroboam and take from the evil to come Abijah for some good thing that was found in him, beholds the few faithful in Sardis and will not suffer them to endure their lot as if they were unnoticed by Him, or allow them to be included in the condemnation of the church to which they belonged."

If we are true to our Christian profession, Jesus pronounces us blessed, and assures us of great reward in heaven, whatever men may think of us. Having kept the garments of grace unsoiled, we shall also wear the garments of glory. And, though excluded from the friendship and society of the proud and consequential on the earth, we nevertheless shall have the sublimer companionship of walking with Jesus in white—in the spotless and trailing robes of dignity and honor.

III. *Notice the specific promises to this church.* "He that overcometh, the same shall be clothed in white raiment."

White is the emblem of perfection, purity, and exaltation. Anciently, when a priest was to be ordained the council examined his genealogy and his person, and if found imperfect he was clothed and veiled in black and sent away; but if all was right he was clothed in white and passed to the dignity of a priest of the Most High. So all Christians are called to be priests of God and of Christ, to serve in the eternal sanctuary. But our attainment to that honor depends on the success of our conflict with sin. If final victors we shall be arrayed in the clean linen, pure and white, as the Lord's royal priests.

The Jewish scribes were ambitious to walk in long robes. They considered it a thing of grace, dignity, and honor. The Roman patricians wore white robes as badges of their high rank which none but themselves might wear. These marked them for the special respect of men and denoted their superior exaltation. Perhaps there were some such in the church of Sardis to whom the people looked up with particular reverence. But better far than all such marks of dignity is the promise to every Christian victor. All such are to be the magnates and patricians of heaven, for Jesus says, "*the same shall be clothed in white raiment.*" The robes of Aaron and the royalty of David, the sacredness of the priests and the rank of kings, shall be united upon them. The successful Christian is to "shine as the sun in the kingdom of the Father"—not simply in what is put on from without, but also with the corresponding inner glorification of the whole being, like that which marked the Saviour on the mount of His transfiguration.

But this is not all. The Saviour further adds: *"And I will not blot out his name out of the book of life."*

When any one submits to become a Christian, and receives baptism into the Christian commonwealth, his name is "written in heaven" as well as in the church-book on earth. There is a celestial roll-book of all those who name the name of Jesus. But it depends on the persevering fidelity of the individual whether his name is to continue on that roll or to be blotted out. There be many names once entered in that book which will not appear there at the final opening of it. There be many whose names were entered there when as infants they were given and dedicated to the Lord who in after years refused to acknowledge and stand to that baptismal consecration, and whose names have long since been erased. There be many whose names were entered there as they gave themselves to be Christ's servants and vowed sacred allegiance to Him until death, but who have so fallen away from their engagements and duties that only blots remain where their names once stood. There be many whose names once glowed with splendid promise in that book of life, but which the tears of the recording angel have expunged because of the apostasies and failures of those from whom so much better things were hoped. And it is a sadness unspeakable to think how many blots and erasures there are upon the books of heaven by reason of the failures of people who once were on the way of life, but dropped out before finishing their race.

But there are names there which never shall be blotted out. They are registered as the true and faithful followers of the Lord, and such they will continue to the end. Though they should be stricken from all the rolls of honor and distinction in this world, they will never be blotted from the Lamb's book of life. Stars may fail, rivers cease to flow, flowers fade, monuments of brass and marble perish, and names which once shook the world die out for ever, but the names of God's persevering saints shall stand in the register of the nobility of heaven, ever brighter and more illustrious as the everlasting ages run. No works and merits of ours can write us in that book, but the all-sufficient grace of Jesus can. And if we have sincerely embraced Him as our Lord and Saviour, and ever cleave to Him as our hope and strength, and continue steadfast in this faith, even *our* unworthy names shall remain upon the book of life as our title to the inheritance of the saints in light.

So far from blotting the name of the Christian victor from the book of life, Jesus further promises, "*I will confess his name before my Father and before His holy angels.*" He requires of us that we confess Him before men. It pertains to true discipleship publicly to espouse Christ's name and cause in the midst of this gainsaying world, and not to be ashamed of the testimony of our Lord. It is the least that we should ever think of doing for Him who has done so much for us. It is the soldier's greatest shame not to stand courageously to his colors. But Christ in turn engages to confess us, to espouse our cause, and to acknowledge and stand for us before God and all the dignitaries of heaven.

It is something to have one's name introduced to the favorable consideration of kings and high potencies, and the higher the dignity and influence of the person presenting us and vouching for us the sublimer is the honor. There is therefore a largeness and blessedness in this promise far beyond what we might on first hearing suppose. It means that the very Son of God, to whom all authority and power in heaven and on earth is given, proposes to present us to the eternal Father as His acknowledged friends, for whom He vouches and for whom He stands, as candidates for enthronement amid the princedoms and sublime fellowships of the heavenly regencies.

And great will be the difference between the names which Jesus will confess in heaven and those which figure so largely in the hearing and annals of men in this world. How many whom popes have canonized and crowds have worshipped will then fail to be mentioned! How many names that have floated down the ages and sounded in endless echoes along the corridors of time as those of the noble, the mighty, the beautiful, and the brave will never once be pronounced or heard in heaven! And how many never known beyond the humblest circles, and never once heard of on earth, shall suddenly come forward to honorable notice as the heirs of eternal dominions to share with Jesus in the kingdom prepared by the Father before the world was! Yes, many names of which all the books and all the newspapers and all the utterances of men now are full shall never once be named there, while others which, like violets by the roadside or like roses in the wilderness, have quite escaped all observation, or which perchance were known only to be contemned and cast out as evil, shall be brought forth as the worthiest and noblest that ever have been worn in this world, and live in sublimer fame for all the everlasting ages than those of the Solomons, the Alexanders, the Cæsars, and the Napoleons in earthly history.

There are names now upon no books on earth but the church-records of some humble congregations which shall then turn out among the highest in the records of the redeemed. There are names of which their owners are half ashamed, and which they never hear pronounced without a degree of confusion as if too uncouth and unworthy to be spoken; but if those who have them will be true and faithful to their Lord and Saviour, and hold out steadfast in their lowly spheres, Jesus will confess them in the Court of heaven, and clothe them with an honor in which they will shine illustrious for ever.

Dear friends, these are very wonderful things, but as true and sure as they are wonderful. Our blessed Lord Himself hath spoken them from heaven, and well do they deserve our careful and believing notation. Not without the most ample reason does He add here also the admonitory words: "*He that hath an ear, let him hear what the Spirit saith unto the churches.*" It is Jesus who speaks, and it is for us to pay the most reverent attention to what comes so direct from the lips of the King. Matters of the weightiest and highest concernment of every man, and especially every Christian, are here brought to our contemplation, and we do but disable and dwarf ourselves by not devoutly taking them to heart. If we are dull and dead in our profession, here is the divine direction what to do about it. If we find the battle hard, the trials heavy, the adversities severe, and the whole tendency of things against us, here is the word to strengthen and encourage us. The strife faithfully maintained will have a glorious issue. The harder the fight, the higher is the heaven to be won. The heavier the cross, the brighter the crown. For the spirit of heaviness come the garments of praise. For our confession of Christ in lowliness will be His confession of us before the Father and His holy angels. We have only to hear and heed and press courageously on, and we need not fear for the result. And when the time comes that the books are opened and the records of the book of life are read out, our names shall be found written in it to our everlasting joy and honor.

"Behold," saith the Saviour, "I give unto you power to tread on serpents and scorpions, and over all the power of the enemy; and nothing shall by any means hurt you. Notwithstanding, in this rejoice not, that the spirits are subject to you; but rather rejoice *because your names are written in heaven*" (Luke 10 : 19, 20).

Lecture Thirteenth.

Rev. 3:7-11: "And to the angel of the church in Philadelphia write: These things saith He that is holy, He that is true, He that hath the key of David, He that openeth, and no man shutteth; and shutteth, and no man openeth: I know thy works: behold, I have set before thee an open door, and no man can shut it: for thou hast a little strength, and hast kept My word, and hast not denied My name. Behold, I will make them of the synagogue of Satan, which say they are Jews, and are not, but do lie; behold, I will make them to come and worship before thy feet, and to know that I have loved thee. Because thou hast kept the word of My patience, I also will keep thee from the hour of temptation, which shall come upon all the world, to try them that dwell upon the earth. Behold, I come quickly: hold that fast which thou hast, that no man take thy crown."

SOME have the idea that there was nothing faulty in connection with the church in Philadelphia, and that its professed members, though weak and poor, were all worthy and commendable Christians. This doubtless was true with respect to the persons included in the Saviour's commendation, but I am persuaded it is a mistake when accepted as covering the whole case.

If the entire professed church in Philadelphia was in such a good condition spiritually, it was an exception to all other known churches; and so is also named at the wrong place in this list, for the order of succession is that of growing deterioration. The few weak ones here so tenderly commended by the Saviour are plainly but a feeble and depressed fraction of the general body of Philadelphians professing to be Christians. There is also a distinct reference to another and more influential class, from whom these few poor saints were suffering much, and whom the Saviour describes as "those which say they are Jews, and are not, but do lie." Who were these? If they were literal born Jews, adhering to their own synagogue, distinct and apart from the professed Church of Christ, it is hard to conceive why the Saviour would say that they were not Jews and that their profession was a lie. The implication also is that if these false ones had been true Jews, as they professed and claimed to be, Christ could and would have approved and commended them the same as the others; whereas this was not possible unless they had been at the same time confessing believers in Him. If the question lay simply between being pseudo-Jews and Jews of the true natural blood of Abraham, Jesus could no more acknowledge them in the one case than in the other apart from Christian faith and profession; so that we are obliged to consider them professing Christians.

It must be borne in mind that a large number of the Christians of those days, in most places, were of Jewish blood. Even Paul, the great apostle of the Gentiles, nearly always began with the Jews, and his first converts were almost invariably from among the Jews. A distinction thus came to be made between believing or baptized Jews and those who stood out in opposition to the Christian faith. Those who believed and were baptized were considered the right Jews—the Jews of the true and saving circumcision of the heart—the Jews who were the only Jews in reality, because they entered into the real faith and spirit of the covenant with believing Abraham; while all others were regarded as spurious Jews, because, while holding to the shell of the ancient faith, they were in fact apostates from the covenant of promise. Hence to profess Christianity was to profess to be the true and only proper Jews according to the genuine spirit and import of the promise to Abraham's seed. This was the doctrine then held.

Accordingly, also, Paul wrote to the Romans that "He is not a Jew which is one outwardly; neither is that circumcision which is outward in the flesh; but he is a Jew [*i. e.* a right Jew] which is one inwardly; and circumcision is that of the heart, in the spirit, and not in the letter; whose praise is not of men, but of God." So also he wrote to the Galatians: "If ye be Christ's, then are ye Abraham's seed, and heirs according to the promise." And had these people been ever so true Jews without being Christians, it is not possible that Christ could have acknowledged and commended them as belonging to His Church.

Those, therefore, whom the Saviour here characterizes as professing to be Jews, but whose profession was a lie, could be none other than persons who professed Christianity, but whose profession was false—so false that He condemns them as a very "synagogue of Satan." The whole description shows that they were the chief body of professed Christians in Philadelphia—people who had things largely in their own control, but were only self-deceivers, hypocrites, and liars, so far departed from all genuine Christianity and so destitute of faith and charity as to be in reality the children of the Evil One—an apostate crew, not at all entitled to place in the congregation of believers.

To confess Christ, to accept baptism into His name, and to take upon us the confession of Christianity are necessary. We cannot be rated as true Christians without these. But mere profession is not enough. We must inwardly be and live what we profess. We must be hearty, true, and consistent in our profession. We must be Christians in reality, and not only in name and claim, in order to have place in Christ's acknowledgment and regard. And it is a sad fact that there be many who make loud and confident claim of being Christians, putting down all others as far beneath them, while their hearts are not at all right; and Christ refuses to acknowledge them as any real part of His Church. Though professedly Christians beyond all Christians, in the view of Heaven they are nothing but a synagogue of Satan, having neither part nor lot with Christ's true people. It is strange that it should be so; that men should so impose upon themselves; that any could be so lost to all right sensibility and honesty as to vaunt themselves as Christians while really the children of the devil. But so it was in this church of Philadelphia, and so it has been over and over again in all the Christian ages; nay, there is every reason for us all to search ourselves well to make sure that such is not our own case.

So, then, this church in Philadelphia, taken as a whole according to profession, was by far the worst in the list thus far. In Ephesus there was a cooling of first love, which is the beginning and source of all that is bad in Christian declension. When the fervor of divine love is gone, the way is open for every other bad development and ill growth. But it was there only a cooling of love. There were some bad practices and some false apostles, but they were vigorously resisted and discipline was maintained.

In Smyrna there were falsifiers who had grown into blasphemers and lying perverters of the truth, who showed that they were of the Satanic school. But they were few and had obtained no standing or control in the church. In Pergamos bad deeds had grown into corrupt doctrines. Errors of life had come to a place in the creed, and falsities began to appear in the place of power and control. The church and the world began to be friends and to intermarry, and the proper distinctness of the church began to be obscured. In Thyatira matters had become still worse. Devil-oracles, sanctioning, teaching, and justifying evil deeds, here found lodgment and place as divine prophecies, and many Christians were betrayed and deceived into the basest uncleannesses under the guise of knowing "the depths of Satan" and triumphing over him by doing his works. In Sardis living faith had come to an almost universal deadness, so that there were but "a few names" left which had not defiled their garments. The Christian profession had been maintained, and there was much formal devotion, but the true spirit of faith had largely departed. The church for the most part had become a mere carcass, beautiful and impressive in external form, with plenty of showy power, winning for it an imposing name, but without life and spiritually dead.

And here in Philadelphia an utterly false Christianity had so far usurped the place of the true that the most influential part of the church could no more be tolerated as at all belonging to the Church of Christ, but was turned into a very synagogue of Satan, overriding, oppressing, and proudly casting out of all sympathy those who alone could be regarded as proper Christians.

It is a melancholy thing to have a name to live and yet be dead or dying, but it is a still worse thing to be alive, active, and potential in what is so contrary to Christ under name and pretence of being the Lord's people. Yet to such deceptions may men persuade themselves, vaunting as pre-eminent children of God while utterly disowned of Christ as none of His. And to this condition had the main body of these Philadelphians reduced themselves.

But there still were some whom the Saviour could and did acknowledge. They were poor, inconsiderable, and at a great disadvantage, but they were believing and true. The pastor seems to have been a weak man and not much esteemed by some of his people, but he was strong enough in faith and principle not to be carried away or silenced by the prevailing majority. He knew the truth, and held it and preached it, though it met with no favorable response or sympathy from the most of his flock. The humbler and poorer ones believed and held with him, but the rest accepted only so much as they liked, held to more liberal ideas, and frowned upon those who were so simple as to take what was taught them as true gospel. But it was true gospel, nevertheless; and the very titles under which the Saviour presents Himself to this church of Philadelphia presuppose some such state of things as I have described.

I. NOTICE THESE TITLES.

"These things saith *He that is holy*"—more literally, "*the Holy One*"—He who is absolute holiness in Himself. This identifies Christ as God, for it would be blasphemy in any mere man or angel so to speak of himself. But the assumption of this title here looks to some unsanctity in the people of Philadelphia with which the Holy One is inherently and eternally at war.

"*He that is true*"—not only true as the truth-lover and the truth-speaker, but the Truth itself—He in whom all truth has its highest and only perfect realization. This again identifies Christ as God. He could not so claim for Himself if He were not God. But the putting of this title forward here points to some intense falsity contemplated in this Letter, and which He is about to treat as absolute truth demands.

"*He that hath the key of David;*" that is, the

key of the divine kingdom to open or shut beyond all other power to reverse it. Such a presentation points to some blasphemous usurpations, some putting of the ban where there was no right to put it, some claim of liberty or authority to open and shut. There was wrong somewhere to be reversed and righted, and an assumption of place, prerogative, or power which was not according to Christ. And hence Christ declares that He has the key— that He will do the opening and the shutting.

All this answers precisely to the representation I have given, that a large part of the professed church at Philadelphia was presumptuously imperious in its apostasy and lying pretensions.

II. NOTICE THE ENCOURAGEMENTS GIVEN.

"*Behold, I have set before thee an open door, and no man can shut it.*" The emphasis is on the *I*, and the clear implication is that some strong human activity was at work to silence these people or to set them back from their rightful place and influence. The announcement is one of encouragement and blessed promise to them. Though men were trying to suppress them and break them down from proclaiming and propagating what they held and believed, the mighty Jesus was with them. He who has the keys of the kingdom was on their side. He who opens and shuts beyond all power of man to make it otherwise, was there to order the course of events, pledging to keep the door open for them in spite of all efforts to hinder or restrain them.

"*Thou hast little strength.*" There was much weakness, so much that they were held to be of little or no account. It was not so much that their strength was unacknowledged, but that it did not exist. Yet in all their weakness and insignificance they had been faithful: "*Thou hast kept My word, and hast not denied My name.*" The particular word which they had kept, and which others denied, is indicated in the tenth verse. Jesus there says, "*Thou hast kept the word of My patience.*" The word of Christ's patience is not only the word of Christ in general, but a more particular word—His word with a special reference. Christ's patience is His forbearance with the wicked, His restraint of summary judgment upon their misdeeds and blasphemies, His keeping of silence for the time under the manifold insults and persecutions rendered to Him and His Church, until the time comes for Him to ascend the throne of judgment and to reward transgressors according to their works. Such a day is coming. God hath appointed it. It is a day that shall burn as an oven, and all the wicked shall be consumed as stubble. It is described as the time when our

God shall no longer keep silence, but shall come with the voice of the archangel and the trump of God to gather all His faithful ones to Himself and to tread the winepress of almighty wrath upon all the children of disobedience. And the word of His patience can be no other word than that of His Gospel with respect to that impending day, when He shall come to rectify all present disorders and to render to every one according to his works.

The keeping of this word of Christ's patience of course includes the keeping of the entire Gospel, but that Gospel as more especially related to His present waiting and forbearance with the wicked till the time for Him to arise and judge the earth—the keeping up of the faith and hope of the Saviour's return, the building of our calculations on it, the conditioning of our behavior with reference to it, the comforting of our souls in it, and the fearless confession and preaching of it as the blessed hope of the saints.

And with such a keeping of the word of Christ's patience the Saviour here credits these poor people as over against their self-consequential contemners, who only ridiculed and despised such ideas and teachings. The cherishing of the advent hope and faith was the central point in their whole Christian character, the highest element of their piety, the chief particular noted in the Saviour's commendation of them. They had kept His word, and above all *the word of His patience*, bearing, forbearing, and holding on in steadfast waiting and looking for the coming again of the Lord Jesus, when all their wrongs should be righted, their confidence vindicated, and all their blessed expectations fulfilled.

And for this, the special favors of Him who is the Holy One, the absolute Truth, and the Possessor of all the keys and powers of the kingdom, were vouchsafed and promised unto them.

Weak and despised as they were, the door was to be kept open for them. Men might try to shut it, but never should succeed in so doing. Christ pledged that He would keep them in place and opportunity, no matter what efforts might be made to decry them or to silence their testimony. They might be held in discredit, contemned, assailed, and denounced, but Jesus engaged to see that they should not be displaced, pulled down, or shut out from position and hearing for their cause. He tells them that He who holds the keys has set an open door before them which no power of man should be able to close.

Furthermore, with all their weakness and disadvantages their cause was to carry in the end. The time was to come when even their opposers and oppressors would come to them in deep humiliation to worship at their feet and to confess that theirs was the true cause of God. The promise meant that the time would come when these haughty despisers in Philadelphia would be compelled to humble themselves to these poor saints, and to confess them after all the true servants and favorites of the Lord. They were on the winning side, and their holding on firmly amid ridicule and detraction was to make of them the very princes of the Lord of hosts. Not by their strength and eloquence, not by their merit and deservings, but by the power and grace of Him who holds all the keys and powers of the kingdom, they were to be brought to honor for holding fast the word of His patience.

Nay more: "*I will keep thee from the hour of temptation which shall come upon all the world.*" There is a time of tribulation coming more severe than has ever been in all the ages. The prelibations of it were experienced under the plagues of Egypt in the days of Moses and during the period in which Jerusalem came to its final desolations. These were the beginnings of the sorrows and trials yet to come on all the unholy dwellers upon earth from one end of it to the other. Christ calls it "*the hour of temptation,*" or *trial*. It will be a brief period, but one of consummated distress and sorrow. It is further spoken of in this book as "*the tribulation, the great one,*" when all the tribes of the earth shall mourn, and judgments upon judgments the most appalling shall fall upon all the children of disobedience. But from these plagues and troubles the Saviour here pledged to save all who keep the word of His patience: "Because thou hast kept the word of My patience, I also will keep thee from the hour of temptation, which shall come upon all the world, to try them that dwell upon the earth."

Nor can there be any doubt as to the way in which He will fulfil this promise. When He was upon earth He gave command to His people, saying, "Take heed to yourselves, lest at any time your hearts be overcharged with surfeiting, and drunkenness, and cares of this life, and so that day come upon you unawares; for as a snare shall it come on all them that dwell on the face of the whole earth. Watch ye therefore, and pray always, that ye may be accounted worthy to *escape all these things that shall come to pass, and to stand before the Son of man*" (Luke 21 : 34–36). Again, He said respecting that same time, "There shall be two in one bed; the one shall be taken, and the other shall be left. Two shall be grinding together; the one shall be taken, and the other left. Two shall be in the field; the one shall be taken, and the other left." And when the question was asked whither these should be "taken," He answered, to where the body is; that is, to where He Himself shall then be, as Paul also explains:

"We"—the true and watching believers—"which are alive and remain shall be caught up to meet the Lord in the air" (Luke 17: 34-37; 1 Thess. 14: 18).

The way, then, in which Christ's true and faithful followers, eagerly waiting for His coming again, are to be kept from the hour of trial and saved from the woes of the great tribulation is by being translated, caught up to heaven, transferred from earth to the presence of their Lord, before the great trial strikes the guilty world. And for this the Scriptures everywhere teach us to look and wait and watch and hope, thus holding fast the word of Christ's patience, sure that if we are thus dutiful and true no fires of judgment shall ever fall upon us, and when the wicked are cut off we shall see it—see it from the pavilion of our security in heaven.

And yet, again, if these poor despised people would only hold fast what they had, they were to be crowned as eternal kings: "*Hold that fast which thou hast, that no man take thy crown.*" It is no mere figure of speech, but the truest and deepest reality, when the promises speak of inheriting the kingdom, wearing crowns, and reigning with Christ for ever and ever. John had a vision of the whole thing when he beheld the indescribable Sitter upon the throne, and round about four-and-twenty other thrones, and upon them four-and-twenty elders seated, clothed in white raiment and having on their heads *crowns of gold*. And again he saw thrones, and they sat upon them, and power to rule was given unto them, and they lived and reigned with Christ.

Dear friends, this is not mere poetry; it is truth. It is not mere pictorial show; it is substantial reality. In the regeneration those who have followed Christ faithfully shall sit on thrones; and when the Chief Shepherd shall appear they shall receive *a crown* of glory that fadeth not away. It is a transcendent promise, but He who makes it is the Truth itself, and has the keys and powers to fulfil it, and will certainly make it good. The poorest, weakest, and most despised saint on earth may yet become an immortal king. There is a crown for him if he will but hold fast the word of Christ's patience amid the wrongs and trials to which he is here subjected.

It will not be long. Jesus says: "Behold, I come quickly: hold fast that which thou hast, that no man take thy crown." That crown is sure to every one if we will but aim for it, continue as we have begun, and hold the beginning of our confidence steadfast unto the end. For this Christ suffered, and died, and ever lives in eternal power, and soon the day of His patience will be over and the glory of His kingdom be revealed. Eighteen hundred years ago the faithful apostle Paul prayed for the Christians of Thessalonica: "The Lord direct your hearts into the love of God, and into a patient waiting for Christ." And this is just what we all need, that we "may be found of Him in peace, without spot, and blameless." Falsities may be thick around us, but we must hold fast, looking for and hasting unto the day when deliverance shall come and glorious triumph. Some may sneer and hold us in disrepute because of our doctrine and our hope, but Jesus bids us hold it fast, and pledges to us support and protection in our fidelity, an open door in this world and an unfading crown in the world to come.

Lecture Fourteenth.

Rev. 3 : 12, 13 : "Him that overcometh, will I make a pillar in the temple of My God, and he shall go no more out : and I will write upon him the name of My God, and the name of the city of My God, which is new Jerusalem, which cometh down out of heaven from My God : and I will write upon him My new name. He that hath an ear, let him hear what the Spirit saith unto the churches."

DISTINGUISHED preacher has said, "There is such a collection of glories gathered together around the head of this Philadelphia church, that I fear lest I should lose myself in the admiration of their much splendor, and forget the soberness of mind which beseemeth the interpreter of God's holy word." Some of these glories, as realized in this world, have already been noticed; but far greater glories, promised to the faithful in the world to come, are now to be considered. And may God help us to treat of them with that reverent and thoughtful soberness which such momentous things demand!

Varied and great is the glory of the promises to the victors in these seven Letters of our Lord. A full and exhaustive treatment of them would fill a volume. They set before us a portion for

Christ's faithful overcomers at which the lean, shadowy, and empty thing which some talk of as heaven sinks into insipidity and contempt. They give us something the soul can take hold of, something substantial and tangible to think of, something fitted to our nature and aspirations, and of a sort to brace up courage manfully to bear the cross that may be laid upon us in this life.

We saw in our last that there is increased evilness in the successive presentations of the seven churches, the first being the best, and each one in its order being a stage or degree deeper in defection than the one before it. But there is likewise a gradation in these promises. Whether the different grades refer to seven orders of saintship or to seven degrees in the rewards of the saints, or to both, there is a distinct rising from glory in the first to higher glory in the second, and so on to the highest in the last. To the Ephesian victor Christ awards restoration to lost paradise, giving him "to eat from off the tree of life which is in the midst of the paradise of God." To him who remained faithful under the Smyrna trials is awarded "the crown of life" and exemption from the second death. To the victor of Pergamos is awarded "the hidden manna, and a white gem engraved with a new name which no one knoweth saving he that receiveth it." The victor of Thyatira is to have authority over the nations, to rule them with a sceptre of iron, and to possess "the morning star." The victor in Sardis has promise of being "clothed in white raiment," to walk with Christ in white, to have his name retained in the book of life, and to be confessed by Christ before the Father and His holy angels. And so there is a still ampler and more manifold promise to the victor of Philadelphia.

Let us, then, note these particulars and endeavor to grasp the depth of their meaning for our edification and encouragement in fighting the good fight of faith.

FIRST ITEM: "*Him that overcometh will I make a pillar in the temple of My God, and he shall go no more out.*"

The *overcomer* here, as in each of the seven Epistles, is the true Christian who holds out faithful to the end against such falsities, errors, evils, and temptations as he may have had to contend with—the true believer, who continues steadfast in his or her faith, and is found waiting and ready when the Lord comes—and specially includes such as keep the word of Christ's patience in humble waiting for His return to right all present wrongs and to bring His true people to their final rewards. And to these overcomers the promise here is that Christ will make them pillars in the temple of God.

But what is the temple thus contemplated? In one sense there is no temple in heaven, and yet in another there is. There will be no movable temple like that erected by Moses. There will be no material and perishable fixed temple like the one built by Solomon. In his vision of the New Jerusalem, John says: "I saw no temple therein." And yet there was a temple, nevertheless, for he immediately adds: "The Lord God Almighty and the Lamb are the temple of it." It is hard for us to conceive of such high things, but in some sense God and the Lamb are a temple to the finally redeemed, where the Saviour and the saved come together in ineffable communion, compassed about by infinite Godhead as a grand eternal temple-enclosure. Meeting, union, worship, oneness, deepest fellowship, hidden in the mysteries, light, and undisturbed manifestations and enjoyments of God and our Saviour, are the main ideas. And into this holy temple the Christian victor is to come as a worshipper, to drink in of this ineffable light, and to share the fulness of this unspeakable beatitude.

Nor only as a worshipper, but as a perpetual dweller, shall the Christian victor come into the heavenly temple; for "*he shall go no more out.*" The temple and the worship and the blessedness and the continuance in it are alike perpetual. As Christ dwells in the Father, so we are to dwell in

Him, with the union and the glory indissoluble for ever. The priests of the earthly temple served by courses. Each course served its time, and then went out. "They truly were many priests, because they were not suffered to continue by reason of death." But it shall not be so with the Christian victor in the eternal temple. Like his Lord, "he continueth ever," and his priesthood passeth not from one to another, for death, infirmity, or need for suspension in the holy service is departed. No sickness shall prostrate him, no labor exhaust his energies, no lapse of time waste his strength, no cause come in for the cessation of the blessed communion. Sweet was the life of our first parents in Paradise, but the time came when they had to leave it and go out to moisten the desert world with their sweat and tears, and find graves under its sod. But from that more glorious paradise restored by the heroism of our blessed Lord there shall be no more such failures, no more such going out. The temple is eternal, the anthems never cease, the worship is never suspended, and the communion is everlasting.

Nor yet as only a permanent dweller in the heavenly temple, but as *a pillar* in it, shall the Christian victor abide.

Pillars are for strength, support, ornament, and commemoration. They are part of the edifice in which they have place. The derivation of the word in Hebrew and Greek seems to contemplate power, dignity, and glory. The Church is called the pillar, support, and upholder of the truth, to give it conspicuity and to keep it in the view of men. Peter, James, and John are spoken of as seeming "pillars" of the Church; that is, its most conspicuous members and strongest supports. And so the victorious saints are to be pillars in the eternal temple, to have place as a part of it. As God and the Lamb are the temple, they are to be joined to God and the Lamb and stand in and with them for ever as dignities, ornaments, and everlasting commemorations of redeeming love and grace, sharing in all the honor and glory of that temple and in the upholding and administration of its services.

God honors His faithful people by resting much of the burden and exhibit of His Name and work upon them already in this world, but a thousand-fold more in the world to come. Man was originally made to be the expression or image of God in the lordship and governing of His earthly creations. What was lost by sin is recovered in still higher forms by redemption. And when the grand restoration is complete and the eternal economies to which redemption looks shall come into place, all glorious with the divine presence, teeming with divine goodness, and working all the divine pleasure, these trophies of grace shall have place in them as pillars in a celestial temple, bearing up its excellent estate, preserving and administering its order, showing forth its glory, and sharing in all its blessed service.

And there their place shall ever be. They shall never move or be severed from the eternal fabric. Other pillars may crumble and fall; the strongest and most admired columns may waste and disappear; the gates of Thebes, the Pyramids of Egypt, and the mightiest architectural monuments in the world may be erased from their places; the very pillars of the earth may be dissolved; but these pillars, which Christ is engaged in building and fashioning amid these years of time, borrowing immortality from decay and splendor from surrounding darkness, shall stand in everlasting strength, beauty, and dignity in the imperishable temple of God and the Lamb.

SECOND ITEM: "*I will write upon him the name of My God.*"

Though Christ is God, yet as Christ He has a God and Father, who through Him is also our God and Father. The name of that God is already put upon us in holy baptism, but it is not so engraved upon us that it may not be rubbed off and cease to be of the significance intended. We are only probationers here, candidates for sublimer prizes when this world is over. And among these future honors and dignities is the permanent engraving upon the final victor of the name of God in all the virtues and immunities which that name can be to an immortal man.

The high priest under the law wore a plate of gold on his forehead, on which there was inscribed, "HOLINESS UNTO THE LORD." It proclaimed his dignity and sacredness—his divine consecration to "bear the iniquity of the holy things which the children of Israel should hallow in all their holy gifts." The same was to be "always upon his forehead, that they might be accepted before the Lord." All this pointed primarily to Jesus Christ as our great High Priest, Sin-bearer, and Intercessor, but likewise also to some eternal consecration of the glorified saints as they are finally joined to the heavenly temple as priests of God. "It doth not yet appear what we shall be; but we know that, when He shall appear, *we shall be like Him;* for we shall see Him as He is."

We are greatly at a loss upon themes so lofty. We see only as through a glass darkly. We know only in part. But it is written of the favored inhabitants of that place where the throne of God and of the Lamb shall be, that they shall serve God and see His face, "*and His Name shall be in their foreheads.*" The dignity of high priesthood, the freedom of unobstructed access to the divine presence, the privilege of looking upon God's face, and all the liberties and prerogatives of admission into the holiest apartments of the eternal temple are certainly implied. As there is nothing which the Name of God does not command or to which it does not admit, so the engraving of that Name upon the people of the Church of the first-born means a guarantee to them of the freedom of all the realm and dwelling-place of God as His acknowledged priests and princes, consecrated for the sublimest offices and services of the world to come.

THIRD ITEM: *"And I will write upon him the name of the city of My God, which is New Jerusalem, which cometh down out of heaven from My God."*

There is a modern sect, heretical as to some of the fundamental doctrines of the faith, and offensively schismatical as to the proper Church of Christ, which has presumptuously and against all right appropriated to itself the title of the New Jerusalem, claiming that their few modern coteries are the true nucleus, centre, and beginning of this sublime city which cometh down from God out of heaven. Unfortunately for the sober truthfulness of any such claim, this so-called New Jerusalem began on earth, sprang from a half-demented nobleman of the earth, who, to his credit, never attempted such an organization, which is altogether of the earth, if not largely from under it. With righteous indignation at such falsifications of God's holy word, and at pretensions which savor more of the beast covered with names of blasphemy than of the inspiration of God which is claimed for them, I warn all whom I can reach and influence to beware of the subtle and good-seeming perversions of the truth by which the father of lies would thus deceive, if possible, the very elect.

The New Jerusalem, the city of God, coming down out of heaven from God and having the glory of God, is not an earthly sect, and the Church of the true New Jerusalem is not an organization of mortal men voicing the vagaries of a diseased imagination as the infallible supplements of the Word of inspired prophets and apostles. The New Jerusalem, God's city, wherein is the throne of God and the Lamb and the issuing waters of life, is a thing of the heavens, God-built and depending for its revelation on the personal coming again of the Lord Jesus to recall from death the sleeping bodies of His saints and fashion them like unto His own glorious body; all of which, in every tenable sense, is totally denied and condemned by the modern sect which proclaims itself the Church of the New Jerusalem.

A city means a city, not a sect. The city

building on earth is Babylon, whose end is destruction; the city building in heaven is the true New Jerusalem, which does not come forth out of the brain of a Swedenborg, but is the embodiment of the glory of God, by Him constructed, by Him brought forth into its place, and possessed only by "the children of the resurrection" when all of this present world is past. Abraham looked for a firmly-founded city whose maker and builder is God. Of the saints of old it stands written, "God hath prepared for them a city." The Christians of Paul's day sought for an abiding city in the world to come. John in his visions beheld that city, that great city, the holy Jerusalem, descending out of heaven from God, with jewels for foundations, gates of pearl, streets of gold, angels for watchmen, and God and the Lamb for its temple and light, arrayed in crystalline glory, in which the saved nations walk, into which nothing that is false or defiling ever enters, which only they inhabit who are written in the Lamb's book of life, and from which they shall reign for ever and ever. And the name of that city of light and glory and manifested Godhead Jesus says He will write upon every one that overcometh, holding fast the word of His patience.

What all that means is more than imagination can conceive or words of man express. Many also may be the questions about it to which in our present clouded and earthy condition we can frame no clear answers. But there is yet to come forth from heaven a new and transcendent commonwealth, with a new and heavenly metropolis, where all the eternal administrations are to be centred in God and the Lamb, and to the full liberties of which, as the princes of the realm, every member of the Church of the first-born is to be sealed and acknowledged when the time for the fulfilment of these promises arrives.

Man was made for heavenly citizenship, possession, rule, and dominion. The universal pursuits of the world and the strongest temptations of the Church in its career on earth do constantly and mightily testify of this. And this great end of creation and redemption, and this unquenchable thirst of the human heart, are to find their consummation in the kingdom to come, especially in its capital city, the New Jerusalem, which cometh forth from God. And the name of that city is to be so engraven upon every victorious saint that there can be no more separation between him and it. His home, his reward, his sublime dignity, and his eternal joy are to be there, full in his possession for ever. Even so, and so precious, is to be the portion of him who keeps the word of Christ's patience and comes off victor in these earthly strifes with error and sin.

FOURTH ITEM: "*I will write upon him My new name.*"

Believers bear the name of Christ now. They are baptized into His Name as the Christ, the Sin-bearer, the Redeemer, the true and anointed Lord and Saviour, in whom all our hopes of forgiveness and eternal life inhere. Before He was born in time it was said, "Call His name JESUS, for He shall save His people from their sins." Nor will He ever lose or lay off this name, for it is ordained "that at the name of JESUS every knee shall bow, of things in heaven, and things in earth, and things under the earth, and every tongue confess that Jesus Christ is Lord, to the glory of God the Father." But in the final accomplishment of all this He will yet take on other names by which He is not now known. When He comes forth in His majesty, with all the armies of heaven following Him on white horses, for the final overthrow of the Beast and the false prophet, He shall have on His vesture and on His thigh a name written, "KING OF KINGS, AND LORD OF LORDS." At the same time He is also to have another name written, "a name that no man knows but He Himself." Whether it is one of these names or some altogether "new name" that He is to engrave upon His triumphant saints, we know not. This only we know, that the time is drawing on when our blessed Lord shall take to Himself some "new name" in connection with some unexplained development in the completion of His grand redemptive purposes, and that He will write that name also upon His victorious saints, thereby uniting them with Himself for ever in whatever dignity, service, or glory that name shall signify.

The riches in Christ Jesus, especially in the purposes and manifestations relating to the finishing up of what is to come hereafter, have not yet been fully revealed. Transcendent things, and in plentiful sufficiency for all our present wants, have been made known to us. There is everything to enlist our faith, command our confidence, and inspire us with transporting hopes. But we do not yet know all. There is much beyond which can only be learned and fully understood when the time for their revelation comes. Yet, whatever these future developments and manifestations may be, or whatever unexplained attitudes our Saviour is yet to take in the ongoing of His purposes in eternity, the pledge here is given by Himself that His saints shall be joined with Him in all. As His present name is on us, sealing to us participation in all that He has achieved and is achieving, so whatever new name He shall assume in the future is likewise to be engraved on His faithful ones, identifying them with Himself in all. Wherever He is, there we are to be.

Whatever He does, we shall have part in. And throughout all the eternal ages and administrations His name shall be our name also, and His lot likewise our lot; for our heirship is conjoint with His own to the eternal patrimony.

Think of the mighty possibilities in the eternal career of Him to whom all power in heaven and earth is given! Think what undescribed demonstrations may yet be manifested in connection with the stupendous scheme of the redemption and regeneration of a fallen world, and what sublime ends in the vast universe the final accomplishment of this masterpiece of the Almighty's doings may be intended to subserve! Think what in the grand purposes of God may be in contemplation with reference to the future of this earth, or thousands of other worlds, or all the boundless realm of living beings of which Christ is to be the centre and the soul! Paul distinctly refers to a mysterious concorporation of worlds and a gathering together of all things in heaven and on earth in one sublime unity in Christ, and of eternal purposes in Christ Jesus our Lord affecting celestial principalities and powers, for which there must come exhibits on His part far beyond all present knowledge and anticipation. And yet in all these unsearchable cycles of manifestation and achievement by our Christ the promise here is that the Church of the first-born, which is His everlasting

Bride, shall share with Him in the kingdom and the power and the glory; for His New Name is to be written on all His victorious people as participant in whatever destiny is before Him in all the ages of the ages.

Verily, dear friends, Jesus has given us "exceeding great and precious promises." In vain do we task ourselves to compass the vastness of their import. Imagination reels and falters, stunned and vanquished, amid the infinitudes of glory and blessedness which they open to our contemplation.

And if such are to be the awards to faith in Jesus and close clinging to Him and His word and directions for the few years we have to live on earth, what is there in all the round of possible things for which we would be justified in letting go our chance to reach them? Well may Heaven speak out its intense sevenfold appeal: *"He that hath an ear to hear, let him hear what the Spirit saith unto the churches."* God help us all to hear and heed, and hold fast the word of our Saviour's patience, that we may not miss a destiny so exalted and which has cost our dear Lord so much!

Lecture Fifteenth.

Rev. 3 : 14 : "And unto the angel of the church of the Laodiceans write: These things saith the Amen, the faithful and true Witness, the beginning of the creation of God."

WE now come to the last of these seven Letters of our Lord. Let us then give attention with prayerfulness of heart and desire to profit. It is our wish to be in accord with the mind and will of our Saviour. What is wrong in us we desire to have corrected. We are anxious to be true Christians, that when the Master comes we may be found of Him without spot and blameless. We know ourselves to be set in the midst of so many trials, temptations, and dangers that we would gladly have some words of comfort, direction, and encouragement from Jesus Himself, that we may be helped and assured in our faith and led into the path of security and eternal life. Nowhere, however, can we find what we need more beautifully set forth than in these Letters from heaven. And this to "the church of the Laodiceans" should specially enlist us, for the reason that it refers more than either of the others to the Church of our times, giving us Christ's judgment of the dangers and duties, the situation and wants, of the Christendom of which we are a part.

These seven addresses were originally made to seven particular churches as then existing, but those churches were selected from among the rest because they so well represented the whole Church from the time of the apostles onward to the end. Hence the command to the people of every age to "hear what the Spirit saith unto the churches." In all time there will be people in the Church answering to the descriptions in these several Letters, who may here see what the Lord's judgment of them is. But while every church has something of these seven churches in it, these utterances of Jesus also indicate the characteristics of seven successive periods in the Church's history, beginning with the time of John and extending to the final consummation. That is to say, they were meant to be prophetic as well as historic, and the course of their fulfilment can be readily traced.

First was the *Ephesian* period—a period of warmth and love and labor for Christ, dating from the apostles, but in which the leaven of evil already began to work, showing itself in the gradual cooling of the love and zeal of some, the false professions of others, and the incoming of undue manifestations of carnal ambition.

Then came the *Smyrna* period—the period of bitterness for the Church in its last severe struggles with heathen Rome, the era of bloody martyrdom and of the sweet savor unto God of faithfulness unto death; but marked also with further elements of defection and departures from the original simplicities of the Gospel, which reached their height during the early part of the fourth century.

Then followed the *Pergamite* period, in which true faith more and more disappeared and clericalism gradually formed itself into a dominating system, and the Church entered into a marriage relation with the powers of this world.

Then came the *Thyatirian* period—the age of purple and glory for the corrupt and ambitious priesthood and of obscuration to the pure evangelic truth—the age of effeminacy and clerical domination, when the Church usurped the place of Christ and many of the true witnesses of Jesus were given to dungeons, stakes, and inquisitions —the age of the enthronement of the false prophetess, whose oppressive dominion extended to the days of Luther and the Reformation.

Then came the *Sardian* period—the age of separation and some vigorous return to the rule of Christ—the age of a new beginning, largely freed from the Balaamitic doctrines, the Nicolaitan tenets, and the fornications of Jezebel—an age of many worthy names that will never die, but withal marked with deadness in its tendencies and developing much to be repented of—an age covering the spiritual lethargy of the Protestant centuries preceding the great evangelical movements of the last hundred years.

Then came the *Philadelphian* era, marked by a closer adherence to the Word in its practical bearings, more fraternity among professed Christians, and a livelier philanthropy toward the suffering and ignorant; but now rapidly giving place to the last phase or period of the Church upon earth, with which its whole history in this world will end and the dispensations of the great judgment take its place.

The *Laodicean* period is therefore that in which we are now living; so that what the Saviour says to the church of the Laodiceans He says particularly to us and to the church-people of our time. Having ears to hear, we should therefore be all the more quickened to hear, mark, learn, and inwardly digest what the Spirit here saith. And may the good Lord help us to hear to our profit and to the saving of our souls from the judgment-disasters which must soon overtake this wicked and unbelieving world!

The particular part of the Saviour's Letter to the church of the Laodiceans now to be considered is His own description of Himself. He had previously described Himself as "He that holdeth the seven stars in His right hand, who walketh in the midst of the seven golden candlesticks;" "The first and the last, which was dead, and is alive;" "He which hath the sharp sword with two edges;" "The Son of God, who hath eyes like unto a flame of fire and feet like fine brass;" "He that hath the seven spirits of God and the seven stars;" "He that is holy, He that is true, He that hath the key of David, He that openeth, and no man shutteth, and shutteth, and no man openeth." Wonderful depths of solemn majesty, experience, office, power, and glory are thus professed and claimed, to which He here adds that He is "*the Amen, the faithful and true Witness, the Beginning of the creation of God.*" And of all the several descriptions this last is the deepest and intensest, and demands our special attention.

Three things does our blessed Saviour thus affirm of Himself:

I. THE AMEN.

"Amen" is one of those peculiarly sacred words reasonably supposed to have originated in heaven. It was constantly on the lips of the Saviour in His most solemn enunciations. Wherever the words "Verily, verily," occur, the original is always *Amen, amen.* From our first meeting with this word in the Scriptures to the end of the Apocalypse, whether on earth or in heaven, it comes before us as a word of intensest sacredness, ratification, and certified reality. It means *So be it*. It is the sealing word to all the Gospels and Epistles. It is not an oath, yet it has much of the solemnity and force of an oath. It contains no adjuration or appeal, yet it authenticates, confirms, binds, seals, and pledges to the truth of that to which it is affixed. Paul says that all the promises of God in Christ are "yea, and in Him amen;" that is, absolutely true, positive, irreversible, and certain over against all that is yea and nay, changeable, doubtful, unreliable, uncertain. The amen of a thing is its unalterable reality concentrated and carried in one brief expression. It is the substantiation of its veriest truth. And when our Saviour thus styles Himself absolutely *the Amen*, He presents Himself to us as the profoundest reality of all revelation and promise—the absolute Confirmer, Ratifier, and Consummator of all pronounced truth—the very Truth of truth.

The exact force of this sublime title has been expressed as "the be-all, and the end-all." And here it is the Be-all and the End-all of the whole purpose of God.

Divine revelation first came in the form of promises, awaiting their fulfilment in future time on certain conditions. Of those promises Christ was the substance, and of those conditions He is the Fulfiller, and so is the Amen of revelation. The promises displayed the goodness, grace, and love of the Father, but the conditions of their fulfilment demanded a perfect righteousness. This no mere man could ever render. Hence no mere man could ever make those promises hold. Firm as they are on God's part, they come to naught by reason of man's impotency and sin. The full obedience being wanting, they could not go into effect. The *amen* to them was still needed, and that amen came in the person and achievements of the Lord Jesus.

Taking the form and place of man, Christ fulfilled the condition of perfect obedience, and thus gave to the promises effective life and availing reality. Only in Him was divine promise sealed unto living effect and ratified for realization. From the beginning until Jesus on the cross said, "It is finished" and entered upon His heavenly dominion, all the sacred utterances of prophet, patriarch, priest, or forerunner of the Messiah were but loose words, like the Sybil's leaves, floating on the winds and tides? It was only when the Christ came, gathered them all together, bound them all up in His own sublime achievements, and made them steadfast in His own blood and triumph, that the effective *Amen* was added to them. Now they are all yea and amen in His ever-living Self, certain and sure in every particular, and can no more fail than He can fail from the majesty of His eternal dominion. All is reality now in Him, for He is *the Amen*

II. THE FAITHFUL AND TRUE WITNESS.

Some have taken this as a mere repetition in another form of what was expressed in calling Himself the Amen. But the glorious Son of God never deals in meaningless tautology. His being the Amen is one thing; His being "the faithful and true Witness" is another; and we must not confound together things that differ.

Christ is the Amen as the substantiator and consummator of all that is promised; He is the faithful and true Witness in the making known to us of the nature, mind, and purposes of God. Hence in the beginning of this book He is called "the faithful Witness" with reference to the revelations given in this book, as given by His authority and on His credibility.

The scriptural conception of a witness is one who gives testimony to what he has seen and knows. In this sense John the Baptist bore witness to Christ, and also said of Him, "He that cometh from heaven is above all, and what He hath seen and heard, that He testifieth." To the same effect Jesus said of Himself, "We speak that we do know, and testify that we have seen" (John

3: 11, 13). Hence also the record of John: "No man hath seen God at any time; the only-begotten Son, which is in the bosom of the Father, He hath declared Him." In these and other like passages Jesus is set forth as the original and sole Witness of all that is known or that can be known of God. Whether the revelation has been in the form of the creation-work, in the form of the Word, or in the form of inward light, it is only through Christ, who is the Utterer and Revealer of God. Thus He is *the Witness* on whom the whole family of man is dependent for what is known or knowable of the will and purposes of the eternal God.

And He is "the *faithful and true* Witness." What He hath seen and knows absolutely He testifies with completest fidelity. He cannot be mistaken, because He testifies what He hath seen, heard, and knows as the Son of God and the only-begotten in the bosom of the Father; and He cannot misrepresent, because He is the Truth itself. All the qualities of a competent, faithful, and true witness thus meet in Him, so that what He witnesseth and speaks can be nothing but the exact truth, on which we may rely with absolute confidence. Christ's word is therefore an infallible word—truth that must stand though the stabilities of heaven and earth should break down and pass away.

III. THE BEGINNING OF THE CREATION OF GOD.

Some have ventured to construe this title in a way to reduce our blessed Lord to the rank of a mere creature, albeit the first and noblest of creatures. But the object for which He Himself introduces it here is to lift our thoughts and conceptions of Him infinitely above all creaturehood. He wishes to have it impressed upon us that in the sentences which He is about to pronounce we have to do with One who has the majesty and power to command and fashion all created things —with One who has done it, even to the bringing of them into being—with One who is the living, active, and personal *principle* whence all things have proceeded and on which all creatures depend.

"The Beginning of the creation of God" is not a part of the creation begun, but that which makes the creation be—not He whom God created first, but He who was the fountain-source of all God's creations, by whom all things were made, and without whom there was not anything made that was made.

Such is the uniform teaching of the Scriptures throughout (see John 1:1-3; 5:19; 1 Cor. 8:6; Col. 1:12-16; Heb. 1:2, 3; Rev. 1:17); and so it must needs be in this place also. Christ is likewise called "the End" as well as "the Beginning," and we might therefore just as legitimately count Him the last and least of creatures as the first and greatest of them. God and Christ are both called Omega, or the End, because they rule and determine the end, which has its principle, root, and spring from them; and so Christ is called Alpha, or the Beginning, from having been the causative Beginner, the living principle, root, and spring of all divine creations. And it is simply impossible to suppose that He who everywhere comes forth to establish His perfect oneness with the Father should here fix an impassable gulf of separation between them.

It is plain, therefore, that Jesus is, and wishes us to regard Him as, verily the Source and Master of all created things, having everything in heaven and on earth under His dominion and control. He would have us understand and know that creation had a beginning, and that He was the Beginner of it. He would have us understand and know that there is a Power back of all the laws of nature, and that He is that Power, as potent in all parts of creation as in the economy of grace and salvation. He would have us understand and know that the Saviour of the world was also its Creator, that all its destiny hangs on Him, and that the time must come when wind and wave shall celebrate His glory and star and flower and gem silently hymn His praise, and all the earth in final retrievement honor His name alike as its Source and its Salvation.

And a great thing it is for us to know and understand these sublime and far-reaching titles of our Lord and Saviour. It is a great thing to know and understand from His own lips that He is the Amen, the Be-all and the End-all, of the sacred promises and prophecies—the Substantiator and Consummator of the gracious proposals of God by fulfilling in Himself all the conditions which seal them into everlasting firmness. It is a great thing to know and understand that He is the faithful and true Witness, and that His testimony concerning all divine things, past, present, or to come, is ever to be relied on as the exact truth, which nothing in time or eternity can change, and which must hold and stand though heaven and earth should pass away. And it is a great thing to know and understand that He is the Beginning of the creation of God—that it is not on an arm of flesh our Christian faith and hopes are built—that the power to save is as unlimited as the power to create—and that in His hands there can be no failure in the fulfilment of His promises or the execution of His threatenings. And as all this He here presents Himself to the church of the Laodiceans and to us, that we may understand with whom we have to do.

Dear friends, have we then so learned Christ? If not, we are not yet in the right of saving faith. We have a great and glorious Saviour, but we need to regard and honor Him according to His testimony of Himself, to think of Him in holiest reverence, to hear and heed His word, and to make sure of being on such terms with Him that He may be to us a gracious Deliverer and not an avenging Judge.

Lecture Sixteenth.

Rev. 3 : 15, 16: "I know thy works, that thou art neither cold nor hot: I would thou wert cold or hot. So then, because thou art lukewarm, and neither cold nor hot, I will spue thee out of My mouth."

T is the Amen, the Truth of truth, our Lord Jesus Himself, who speaks these solemn words. They are addressed to the angel, or pastor, of the church in Laodicea. They express the mind of the infallible Judge with regard to the spiritual condition of this man and of the church to which he ministered.

Very high authority asserts that Archippus, whom Paul called his fellow-soldier, was the person here addressed. If such be the fact, we find certain doubts about him before this. The apostle Paul sent a message to him by the Colossians to the effect: "Say to Archippus, Take heed to the ministry which thou hast received in the Lord, that thou fulfil it." This suggests that the apostle was not quite satisfied as to the persevering fervor and fidelity of this man in the duties of his office. At the same time he told the Colossians of some "great conflict," some anxious misgiv·

ing, he had "for them at Laodicea;" which indicates not only his great interest in them, but that the tendency of things there was not altogether what it should have been. And here, in this Letter, the Saviour Himself gives judgment that both pastor and people were alike very deficient in the deeper spiritual elements of religion, and that, with all their wealth and outward prosperity, there was nothing to be said in commendation of their spiritual condition.

In the verses now before us three states or phases of life with respect to Christianity are described, accompanied with indications of the divine mind and judgment with regard to them:

    I. A STATE OF COLDNESS;
    II. A STATE OF WARMTH;
    III. A STATE OF LUKEWARMNESS.

I. What, then, are we to understand by the state of *coldness?* The language is figurative, and must be interpreted accordingly; but there is no need that we should dwell long on explanations. *Cold* describes a negative condition; it is simply the absence of heat. And to be in a state of coldness with regard to Christian life, duty, and experience is to be in a condition untouched by the powers of grace. It describes those quite outside of the kingdom of God—those who have never heard the Gospel—those who make no profession of faith in it—those having no pretensions to Christian life and experience. Of this class were the publicans and harlots in the days of Christ.

There are always and everywhere very many of this class. We all know of people who care nothing for religion, pay no attention to it, live as if it were nothing but fable, priestcraft, and superstition, and stand aloof from the Church and all Christian associations and obligations. All such are "*cold.*" They are said to be cold, because they have never been warmed by Christian truth, never been moved to Christian life, profession, or endeavor, and live along in the spiritual deadness of carnal nature without regard to any claims of God or any attempt to avail themselves of the offers that come forth through the Gospel.

We are also very well assured that this is not at all a state which the great Judge approves or in which He wishes people to be. The whole purpose for which Christ came into the world, suffered, died, rose again, appointed His Church, commissioned His ministers, and sent forth His Word and Spirit is to bring people out of their dead coldness in sin and to warm them into animate and living children of the living God. The Scriptures everywhere assure us that those who abide in this *coldness* are in a state of death and condemnation, and that until they are touched, warmed, and quickened by the powers of divine grace, and animated to living faith and Gospel obedience, the wrath of God abideth on them.

II. It is therefore easy to see also what it is to be in a state of *warmth*. It is the opposite of coldness. We have a marked instance of it in the change wrought in the sardonic Zaccheus. He was a bad man, and so was very *cold;* but he was warmed. When he encountered the holy love and tender sympathy and moving look and gracious words of Him who came to seek and to save that which was lost, he was touched and deeply affected. He was made to feel that he was not only hated and despised, but that there was consideration and hope for even so great a sinner as he had been. His morose and avaricious heart opened to the presentations of a new spirit which drove out of him his old bitterness and revengeful injustice, so that the acrid waters of his soul began to clear in the calm sunshine of heavenly purity and affection. He began to see and realize the blessed Saviour's character and mission as never before, and he became alive to it. The heavenly goodness took hold of him, moved him, and so warmed him toward itself that he at once set about making restitution to those whom he had wronged, welcomed the merciful Jesus as his guest, and became a child of God to whose hard heart and godless home salvation had come. From utter coldness he had become warm.

It was the same in the case of Saul of Tarsus. He was very bitter cold toward Christ, but he became entirely changed. Convinced and moved by the vision and word of Jesus, he turned from his malignant hatred and persecution, submitted to the despised Nazarene as his Lord and Saviour, and set himself to serve the Master with a zeal and earnestness which nothing could cool or turn. He even counted all things but refuse that he might serve Christ and finish his course with acceptance to the glorious Redeemer whose cause he espoused. He was completely *warmed*.

So it was with the patriarchs, who received the promises and were persuaded of them, and embraced them, and confessed that they were strangers and pilgrims on the earth, looking for an abiding city whose maker and builder is God.

So it was with Moses, who chose rather to suffer affliction with the people of God than to enjoy the pleasures of sin for a season, and ever endured as seeing Him who is invisible.

So it was with the prophets, apostles, and holy martyrs, and hundreds and thousands in every age, who forsook the ways of the wicked and joyed to cleave to the testimony of God against all hindrances and sufferings, if that by any means they might attain to the better resurrection.

And so it is still with those who hear the word, and in good and honest hearts keep it and make it their meat and drink to do the will of the Father which is in heaven. All these, though once cold, came to be of the company and congregation of the *warm*, whose hearts were touched and kindled with the love of God, and whose whole nature was made to glow with zeal and fervency in their high calling of God in Christ Jesus.

Nor can there be any doubt as to how those in such a state of mind and heart are regarded by the great Judge. It is to all such that the promise is, "Fear not, little flock; for it is your Father's good pleasure to give you the kingdom."

III. But the Saviour here speaks of still another state or phase of life respecting Christianity—a state in which there is neither cold nor heat, but a condition intermediate between the two—a state of *lukewarmness*. What, then, is this?

One who is lukewarm is one who has been partially warmed, and is no longer in a state of coldness. If coldness denotes a condition where grace has made no impression at all, a state of total deadness to Christian influences and requirements, then *lukewarmness* must denote a condition in which there has been some kindling to divine truth, some warming to the presentations of the Gospel, and a partial answering to its calls and claims.

To be lukewarm a man must be *partly warm*. The powers of grace must have made some perceptible impression upon him. He must be in some measure a Christian, interested in sacred matters, and somewhat on in Christian profession and life. There must be something of Christianity in him, or he would have no warmth at all, and hence could not be said to be lukewarm.

All the persons addressed in the text were professed believers. They had taken upon them the Christian profession. They had been baptized and had accepted position as members of the Church. They confessed Christ as their Saviour, wore the badge of discipleship, and had ranged themselves in the line of Christian obedience and duty. Otherwise they could not have been rated as part and parcel of the church in Laodicea. Nor were they without a degree of seriousness in the matter, or they could not have been spoken of as partially warm. And yet they were not up to the standard of earnestness, zeal, devotion. and faithfulness to entitle them to be considered true and consistent members of Christ.

Now, there are very many ways in which people may be partial Christians, largely under the influence of Christianity, and rated with the pious part of the community, while yet very far from being such Christians as Christ can accept and approve.

Many consider themselves Christians, and Christians of the better sort, who are quite indifferent to the doctrines they hold. They make nothing of creed, despise it, and want nothing to do with those who are in any wise strict and earnest about it. If only people will be good, virtuous, charitable, and kind to everybody, they think the great thing in religion has been reached, no matter what they believe or to what sort of creed they hold. Their religion is a mere goodishness, which has something of moral warmth in it, but which when tested is only a tepid sentimentalism, having nothing of the solid backbone of Christianity in it.

Others are very rigid and punctilious about sound doctrine. They make orthodoxy everything, and are ready to fight and suffer for it, but are not so particular about their lives. They stickle earnestly for the creed and the unadulterated truth; and so far they are warm. But when it comes to orthodoxy of practical godliness, they are anything but warm, and hence must be classed with the lukewarm.

Some have right enough views of things, and feel quite properly with regard to all the claims and requirements of Christianity, and are ready enough to confess to their whole duty, being full also of serious self-promises to conform to what they acknowledge. And so far they also are warm, and show it in many ways. But they never come to the point of making full surrender and honest endeavor to live up to their knowledge and persuasions. They have some Christian warmth, but they are only half warm.

Many, again, are given to a divided worship and affection. Like the ancient Jews, they worship Jehovah, but serve other gods. Their devotion is divided between God and Mammon, between Christ and the world, between living for heaven and living for self and earthly vanities and gains. In some respects they are warm enough Christians, but the warmth is neutralized by their constant adventures into a temperature in which there is nothing of Christ or Christianity, and where true piety cools and dies. All their warmth is but *lukewarmness*.

Of all states in which any one living can be, this is the worst. The Saviour here contemplates a complete coldness as less unfortunate than a mere milk-and-water Christianity: "*I would that thou wert cold or hot.*" And the reasons are obvious. Something may be made of the *cold*, and there is something of eternal worth in being *hot*, but to be neither one nor the other is sickening and next thing to hopeless. If the warmth amounts merely to lukewarmness, nothing in the world can be made of it; and those who have reached it and habituated themselves to rest in it are worse off than those who have never been reached by the powers of grace. They certainly are in a less favorable condition to become thorough Christians or to be brought to ultimate salvation. To be religious without true piety, to be captivated and pleased with a profession which does not carry with it the whole heart and life, to count on heaven because we are so much better than the totally cold and unbelieving, while yet not up to the standard of consistent Christian faithfulness, shows a lack of honest sincerity; and a lack of candor is more in the way of thorough conversion to God than candid and undisguised unbelief. A Saul of Tarsus may be a great sinner, but, being honest in his wrong, there is some moral leverage left by which to bring him to a better life. But a man who feels himself virtuous, warm, and far enough advanced to be cherishing hopes of salvation, though really only lukewarm, never takes to himself those truths and arguments by which the impenitent, unbelieving, and cold may perchance be awakened and converted. Efforts made to bring him right he is disposed to resent as impertinence. Is he not a Christian? Has he not taken up the cross to follow Jesus? Does he not believe and confess and worship with the congregation of the Lord? And so he is beyond the reach of conviction. Besides, there is an offensive inconsistency in willingly accepting so much, and resting in it with self-satisfaction without going the whole length, which grieves away those operations of the Holy Ghost without which no one can come to saving warmth. It is an offence to the Lord Jesus. And hence the fearful threat of the text: "*So then because thou art lukewarm, and neither cold nor hot, I will spue thee out of my mouth.*"

A lukewarm Christian, then, is not yet a saved man. He may be on the way to salvation, and lack but little to bring him to eternal life, provided he warms on into the full life of faith. No one is hot from the start. There are many degrees from cold to hot, and every Christian must pass through them all, including the stage of lukewarmness also. But to stop there, counting that we have come to saving warmth while only lukewarm, and thinking ourselves Christians when we are only half-Christians, is to put ourselves in a condition more dangerous and more certain of failure than if we had never tasted of the heavenly gift and never felt anything of the constraining power of the truth. There is more hope for the conversion and salvation of an honest atheist than for a spoiled, half-hearted, conceited, and self-deceived religionist. The publicans and harlots can more readily be brought into the kingdom of heaven than the sanctimonious Pharisees with their much fasting and long prayers and loud thanksgiving for their supposed saintship.

The lukewarm Christian is a self-satisfied person. He feels that he is no longer subject to the shocks and charges which the law fulminates against the wicked. He is just warm and comfortable enough to let all the awakening terrors of the Lord fly past him. He has come so far in the line of goodness and faith that he feels quite sheltered from the dreadful liabilities which hang over the cold and irreligious. He has come just far enough to be self-secure, and so it is next to impossible to reach him and bring him right. The man who knows himself to be a sinner, and that he has not accepted Christ as his Saviour, may yet one day fall at the Redeemer's feet. The waves of trouble may yet make him cry to be led to the Rock that is higher than he. But the self-flattered and self-satisfied half-Christian thinks he has all he needs, and cannot be so readily impressed, awakened, and moved with a sense of what his case requires. If he were *cold*, something could perhaps be done with him; and if he were *hot*, he would not settle down in such indolent self-complacency; but as he is *lukewarm*, there is little hope for him, except to be vomited out of the Saviour's mouth and rejected as a sickening and incorrigible nondescript.

Dear friends, these are very solemn truths, and we must not put them from us as if they did not concern us. Perhaps there never was a time in which there was so much half-hearted and self-satisfied religion as in our day. There is an immense amount of goodishness which passes for Christianity, and which greatly enlists the zeal of many, but which is only a mixture of half and half, neither the one thing nor the other. It is not irreligion, for it has much in it that belongs to genuine godliness; but neither is it out-and-out the religion of the Gospel, and multitudes are deceiving themselves by it to their everlasting discomfiture.

I have said that the Letter to the Laodiceans applies pre-eminently to the Church of our times, and we have only to look at the condition of our churches to see that this neither-cold-nor-hot state completely characterizes the vast body of what is called the religious part of modern Christendom. Of course there are some good and true Christians whose hearts are warm and who are living up to their profession the best they can. Not every member of the church of Laodicea was only lukewarm. It is hardly possible for a church—if it be a church at all—to become so weak and worldly as not to have in it some in whom the germs of living faith survive. The dreariest and most barren deserts have here and there some show of life and some feeble, struggling flowers. Where God's word sounds the assurance is that it shall not return utterly void. Some, in the simplicity of their hearts, will believe it and live upon it as the true children of the Father. So long as the Church of Christ endures there will be some in it who are faithful and true. And when the Saviour spoke of the church in Laodicea as "neither cold nor hot," He did not mean every individual member of it personally. He spoke only of the prevailing condition of it as a whole—its general state as brought out in the sentiments, feelings, life, and character of its most representative people. What He says is that there was far more lukewarmness and neither-hot-nor-cold religion among them than there was of sincere, earnest, and devoted Christianity—that in the mass there were a great many more half-worldly and only half-Christian people among them than of any other class. And just so it is now. It is not that there is no respect for religion; no zealous profession; no holding to the Gospel as of God and the only hope of man; no liberal giving and doing for the honor and dignity of the Church and its institutions; no loud and pretentious activity in what people call Christianity; no ready enrollment of multitudes who confess Christ. In all these respects there is much of which the Church of our day is disposed to boast itself against the state of things in other times and ages. But the point is, that with all this there is such a mixing up of worldliness, worldly feeling, worldly living, worldly thoughts and policies, and a worldly pride and self-satisfaction, that in the vast majority of those who count themselves Christians the religious temper and life stand at an average of neither cold nor hot; which is sickening to Christ and fast tending to an utter rejection from His acknowledgment. And if we, dear friends, are disposed to be satisfied with ourselves and our attainments in grace, with no burning desire to improve upon our Christian life and devotion, then are we of that same neither-hot-nor-cold class, and must begin our work over again, lest we be utterly rejected by our Lord.

Lecture Seventeenth.

Rev. 3 : 17, 18: "Because thou sayest, I am rich, and increased with goods, and have need of nothing; and knowest not that thou art wretched, and miserable, and poor, and blind, and naked: I counsel thee to buy of Me gold tried in the fire, that thou mayest be rich; and white raiment, that thou mayest be clothed, and that the shame of thy nakedness do not appear; and anoint thine eyes with eye-salve, that thou mayest see."

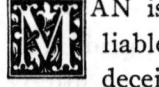AN is very liable to be deceived, and as liable to deceive himself as he is to be deceived by others. People deceive themselves as to their personal attractions, their mental powers, and the credit to which they think themselves entitled; and they can just as readily deceive and impose upon themselves with regard to their spiritual estate and moral qualities. A very marked instance of this presented itself in the case of this church at Laodicea.

It is hard to conceive how these people could be so confident in their good thinking of themselves when the facts were just the contrary of what they supposed. We would think that persons so lukewarm and worldly as they would show some degree of reserve and diffidence in supposing themselves full up to every requirement and in need of nothing. But in proportion to their lukewarmness was their self-satisfaction and their confidence that they were quite rich in every needful good. "Having reached a sufficiency for all that they were inclined to, they persuaded themselves that they had all that they were bound to," and so considered that they were amply enriched beyond all further danger or want.

Interpreters have questioned whether the riches in this case are to be taken as worldly or as spiritual riches. Both doubtless were in the Saviour's mind. Laodicea was a rich city, perhaps the most famous wool-market in the world. Many of the products of the East there exchanged hands for distribution toward the West, leaving rich profits for the Laodicean merchants and manufacturers. There is reason to believe that the church there was the wealthiest in earthly goods of any then existing. And where there is great wealth there is apt to be a great deal of self-confidence. The rich are prone to think themselves pretty well fixed and guarded against all peradventures. There is great power in great wealth, and a church made up of wealthy members is easily persuaded that it has everything necessary to answer all possible purposes.

But with their temporal riches these people connected spiritual riches also. They had an idea of wealth in grace, and some persuasion that there was no want of that in which Jesus says they were poor. The bad feature of the case was that they were self-deceived. They could not have been so grossly deceived as to suppose themselves rich and increased with worldly goods if really poor in that respect. Their false opinion of their riches must therefore have included some thought of spiritual riches, however much it may have been begotten by their worldly plenty. Rich in the things of this world, they considered themselves well off in grace too, and were so well pleased with their whole estate that they could not see that they had need of anything, whether in reference to their Christianity or their outward condition. Nay, the ultimate stress of the description falls upon spiritual matters, implying that these people were walking in a vain imagination of their good estate toward God, not knowing that their self-sufficiency was an egregious self-delusion.

But whether their boastful conceit had reference to their temporal wealth, their spiritual wealth, or both, there was a very wide difference between Christ's estimate of them and their estimate of themselves. *They* thought they were rich; *He* says they were poor. *They* doted on their increase in everything to make them happy; *He* says they were in a condition of wretchedness and misery without knowing it. *They* were satisfied and persuaded that they had need of nothing; *He* says they were destitute, blind, and naked. They had no sense of the reality of their condition, no just views of God or themselves, no right perception of the ways of life and the requirements of salvation. *They were miserably deceived.*

If it was their worldly prosperity in which they commended themselves, they were in dread mistake to suppose that earthly goods would avail them before God or carry them safely through the day of judgment. Dives was a rich man, clothed in purple and fine linen, and fared sumptuously every day; but "he died, and in hell he lifted up his eyes, being in torments." And if it was their supposed spiritual riches, they were equally mistaken in expecting heaven on a mere lukewarm and halfway Christianity. It is not what we think we are that determines our estate, for it may be all delusion. Nor are we what others may say we are, for it may be their ignorance, their malignity, or their flattery. But we are what God sees us to be, whatever thoughts or calculations to the contrary we may indulge.

How these people came to entertain such false conclusions in reference to their good estate is indicated in the fact stated in the preceding verses. They were neither cold nor hot, but lukewarm. If cold and wholly outside of the influences of religion, they could not have counted themselves so secure and well off before God, nor have felt themselves warranted in indulging Christian hopes. But they were half warmed in spiritual things. They had gone far enough in Christianity to make them think and feel that they were Christians. What were they if they were not Christians? They were not heathen, they were not Jews, and, if anything, they must needs be Christians. And being Christians, and so rich, why should they not consider themselves admirably well off for both worlds? If they had been hot and entered fully into the Christian spirit and life, they would have had no confidence in the flesh, and, like Paul, would not have counted that they had apprehended all for which they were apprehended of Christ. But they were *lukewarm*, and their lukewarmness made them dull and indifferent in self-examination. They were not hot in Christianity, and hence not anxious enough about their spiritual condition to search themselves well in the light of God's truth; and their lack of proper self-examination left them to the false inference that as they were outwardly prosperous all was right with them spiritually. Nay, how could it be that they were not in the highest standing with God, seeing that He had so greatly blessed them? It was doubtless in some such way that they reasoned. And so they concluded that they were in all respects well off and happy, not knowing or suspecting that they were really in a state of miserable poverty, blindness, and nakedness.

It is sad to think that even as Christians we are liable to such dreadful deception; but so it is, and we cannot alter it. And such self-deception is sure to come and take possession of us if we allow ourselves to settle down contentedly in a lukewarm and halfway Christianity. To cultivate just enough religion to keep us easy in conscience, yet not enough to keep us uneasy and anxious about our salvation, exposes us to the greatest danger and opens the door for this miserable Laodicean condition of thinking ourselves rich and needing nothing while still in pitiable lack and destitution. The urgent necessity is ever upon us, if we would indeed come to eternal life, to search ourselves often and thoroughly lest we should become the victims of this very delusion.

Notice, then, what the Amen, the faithful and true Witness, says, by way of requirement and direction in the case of these lukewarm, self-secure, and self-deceived people. The words are plain and pointed, and apply to all who think they stand, as well as to those originally addressed: *"Because thou sayest, I am rich, and increased with goods, and have need of nothing; and knowest not that thou art wretched, and miserable, and poor, and blind, and naked: I counsel thee—"*

"I *counsel* thee." There is a tinge of irony in

the way the Saviour speaks, though an irony of love for the good of those addressed. He who might have commanded gives "*counsel*," and conforms His manner of speech to the conceit of the persons addressed. They were very great and high people in their own esteem—so great and high that it was scarce in place to address them as common sinners. They were rich and wise, and hence to be very deferentially approached. And so the Saviour uses the dialect pertaining to their conceited dignity and self-consequence. It was not for them to be spoken to in the tone of rebuke and imperial command, and so He suggests to them a piece of *counsel* which they might perhaps condescend to consider.

What, then, did He counsel? "I counsel thee to *buy of Me gold tried in the fire, that thou mayest be rich; and white raiment, that thou mayest be clothed, and that the shame of thy nakedness do not appear; and anoint thine eyes with eye-salve, that thou mayest see.*" And a deep-cutting counsel it was.

They were people of business and large buyers of all the products coming from the East, that they might sell them again at high advances to the consumers of the West. And so the Saviour suggests and counsels whether they had not better consider the propriety of doing a larger business with *Him*, and take some stock in the treasures and wares which He had to dispose of: "*I counsel thee to buy of Me.*"

They had accumulated goodly fortunes. They were rich and plentiful in gold. But their gold was not such gold as would maintain its proper weight when tried in the balances of judgment. It was gold only half refined, that would not pass at all for currency in the kingdom of God. He had the true gold, the tried gold, the genuine and pure coin, which whosoever hath is rich indeed, and can travel or dwell at liberty in all realms.

Everywhere do we read of the riches of Christ, the true riches, the treasures that make rich toward God—treasures which moth doth not corrupt and thieves can never steal. These are made up of the only pure gold, the only riches that can give rank and place in the heavenly commonwealth. And the counsel here given by the Saviour is that it would be to the advantage of these buyers to try to come to terms with Him to possess themselves of the pure and abiding riches.

As many came from the far East to Laodicea with their camels laden with wools, fabrics, and treasures to sell to these merchants, so Christ here represents Himself as having come to them with all the precious things of His kingdom, proposing that they should buy of Him the genuine goods which should be to them the treasures of refined gold, current for all wants, even to life eternal.

Many of these people were traders in wool and garments and articles made of wool. The raven-black wools of Laodicea were famous throughout the world. But they were not of such sort as to serve for the clothing and covering of the nakedness of the soul. Therefore the Saviour counsels them to buy raiment from Him—not black raiment such as theirs, but *white* raiment—raiment that would serve to array them for the society of heaven. We read many times of the fine linen, white and clean, which is the righteousness of the saints—of robes made white in the blood of the Lamb, of garments unspotted by the flesh, of being clothed with righteousness and with the garments of salvation. And this is the raiment that Jesus proposed that these people should buy of Him.

Some of these were large dealers in ointments, perfumeries, and medicines, brought from various places noted for their production, and highly valued for their healing virtues. But such ointments and oils as they handled could not heal spiritual ailments. Among them all there was no eye-salve that could cure their distorted vision or recover them to right views of their real condition and wants. They believed, and as believers they had membership and place in the Church, but they had not added to their faith virtue, and to virtue knowledge, and to knowledge temperance, and so on to the fulness of Christian life and vigor, and hence were blind and could not see properly, and needed an effective eye-salve which Jesus proposed to furnish. Indeed, He came for this very purpose, to open blind eyes and remedy the obscured and misleading vision of the children of men. Hence He counsels these easy-going and self-complacent people to get His eye-salve and anoint their eyes with it, that they might see; for only the unction from the Holy One can ever give clear-sightedness to perceive the truth, and thus to become wise unto salvation.

These things Jesus counselled these people to *buy* of Him. But how can wretched, miserable, poor, blind, and naked people *buy* anything? The counsel looks like a self-contradiction and an impossibility. But the *buying* of which He counsels is the buying Isaiah speaks of, where it is said, "Every one, and he that hath no money, come ye, buy and eat: yea come, buy wine and milk without money and without price." There is dealing with Christ required, and there is something of price demanded, but it is not beyond the reach of the poorest. Nay, the deeper the consciousness of destitution and poverty the better the chance for a successful purchase. The word is, "To this man will I look, even to him that is poor, and of a contrite spirit, and trembleth at My word." All who really wish to have the

Saviour's fine gold and white raiment and healing unction, and apply to Him for them, and covet them earnestly, and open their mouths wide unto Him, are already in the way of possessing them. Only "let the wicked forsake his way, and the unrighteous man his thoughts, and return unto the Lord, and He will have mercy upon him, and to our God, for He will abundantly pardon." But people must renounce the world and its follies. They must let go their conceit and good opinion of themselves. Whatever of peace and prosperity may have come to them, they must never think they have sufficiently attained, nor give place to the delusion that they are rich, and so increased with goods as to be in want of nothing more. They need to feel and know that of themselves they are never other than wretched, and miserable, and poor, and blind, and naked, and hence need to put themselves in close and constant communication and dealing with Christ, who is prepared and ever ready to enrich them with the pure gold, to clothe them with the white raiment of His righteousness, and to anoint them with the healing and rectifying unction of His Holy Spirit.

There is particular emphasis laid on the words "*of Me.*" These Laodiceans were very ardent and active in trying to enrich themselves by buying of other people, but they were not so much concerned to enrich themselves with the pure and immortal riches to be had only of *Him*. The counsel, therefore, was for them to transfer to *Him* the activity and earnestness of dealing which characterized their transactions with other comers. No one can ever get and enjoy the true riches if he is not willing to deal with Christ. He is the possessor and administrator of all saving grace. No one can have salvation and leave Him out. Every one must go to Him, buy of Him, and have constantly to do with Him, or all hopes must fail. Declining to deal with Christ or to come to terms with Him, we decline heaven, and must remain poor, naked, and wretched for ever; for no one has the riches and goods and medicines we need but Himself. There is none other name given under heaven among men whereby we can be saved. In Him are all the treasures of wisdom and knowledge. In Him are the only life and light of the children of men. "He that believeth on the Son hath everlasting life; and he that believeth not the Son, shall not see life, and the wrath of God abideth upon him." Whether for the cold or for the lukewarm there is no other way out of our poverty and wretchedness but to come to Christ and buy of *Him*. Our salvation is in His merchandise.

And a blessed thing it is that He comes to us with His precious treasures and proposes to make them ours. We have not to go far to find Him. He comes to us. A great way has He travelled to reach us, and at great cost has He procured for us the pure gold, the raiment of justifying righteousness, and the unction of permanent healing for all defects. He also invites us to come and buy, ready to pass all into our possession on the spot if we desire them. And His terms are very easy. We have only to cease resting on our own sufficiency, turn from all other hope, and take the treasures which He offers. We can have them for the taking.

Dear friends, a great and costly opportunity is ours. Let us not think that we have no occasion to embrace it. Let us not think that we are rich and increased with goods and have need of nothing. Let us not suppose because we have taken upon us the Christian profession, and have been much favored with the sunshine of prosperity, that we are anything but poor, needy sinners. We only deceive ourselves if we do. Every day, every hour, we need the Saviour's atoning blood and gracious forgiveness. We stand continually in shameful nakedness till clothed with His righteousness. We are all the time full of blindness, ailment, and folly, which His grace alone can heal. We are as much in want to-day as ever we have been in our lives. Our Saviour knows this, and what a wretched self-deception it is for us to think otherwise! Accordingly, He comes to us laden with His precious goods, that we may buy of Him, and never think ourselves rich and happy except as we again and again renew and keep up our commerce with Him. And here in the text He stands before each one of us to-day, telling us of our poverty and wretchedness, and counselling us to buy of Him gold tried in the fire that we may be rich, and white raiment that we may be clothed, and the healing salves of heavenly unction that we may be cured of our great infirmities. Let us, then, be thankful for our chance, and earnestly embrace it while we may.

Lecture Eighteenth.

Rev. 3:19: "As many as I love, I rebuke and chasten: be zealous therefore, and repent."

WHAT is written in Proverbs (3:11, 12) as pertaining to God, Jesus here quotes as pertaining to Himself. The explanation is found in that saying of His: "*I and My Father are one.*" If the Father loves and chastens, the Son loves and chastens; and if the Son loves and chastens, it is the Father doing it, for the Father is in the Son and the Son in the Father, and the administration in either case is one and the same.

That God in Christ is supremely good and benevolent is evidenced on all hands. That He exercises a very tender affection for His creature man, and is very loving to those whom He has chosen, is declared in all the Scriptures. But what is here announced as His way of dealing with the objects of His regard appears a little strange and paradoxical to natural expectation. We would rather suppose that those whom God loves He would make rich and great and noble and renowned, that He would give them all the world can afford, and that He would show His favor by wreathing their brows with honors that do not fade and filling their coffers with riches that thieves cannot steal. It was somewhat in this way that these Laodiceans reasoned. But the Saviour speaks very differently. He here gives it as the settled principle of His administrations that those whose lives are flowing on amid sunshine and flowers have most reason to doubt their favorable standing with Him, for as many as He loves He rebukes and chastens. The builder does not touch the stones which he has not chosen for place in his edifice. He deals only with those which he most approves and intends for the most honored places; and these he hews and chisels and rasps to shape and fit them for their positions.

To rebuke (ἐλέγχω) is to reprove, to convict, to shame, to show one his errors. *To chasten* (παιδευω) is to teach and educate by means of the rod, to correct with severity, to punish for the cure of wrong, to set right by scourging, as in the case of a father dealing with a child. The two are run together and describe severe disciplinary treatment, meant to suppress and remove faults and imperfections and to bring about a bettered condition. The words designate a painful and humiliating treatment, not to destroy, but to educate, correct, develop, improve, and fashion to propriety, honor, and goodness. And so the Saviour says He deals with all whom He loves.

The whole history of the Church from the beginning until now is one continuous illustration of the statement, "As many as I love I rebuke and chasten." From Abel, who died a martyr within sight of lost Paradise, and from the tears of Adam and Eve over his untimely and tragic death, down to the latest sorrows in the homes of the saints, the truth stands out that as many as Jesus loves He rebukes and chastens. The rule admits of no exceptions. No one is exempt from its operation. The devil may promise worldly prosperity to his children, but Jesus says we must enter the kingdom of heaven through much tribulation. Where His loving favor rests, there it is part of the administration of His love to deal out corrective discipline. If we are not chastened betimes, we are not the subjects of His grace; "for whom the Lord loveth He chasteneth, and scourgeth every son whom He receiveth. If ye endure chastening, God dealeth with you as with sons; for what son is he whom the father chasteneth not? But if ye be without chastisement, whereof all are partakers, then are ye bastards, and not sons" (Heb. 12 : 5-8). And as those who are not scourged are not legitimate children, so those who are not rebuked and chastened are not loved.

Very precious also is this discipline of suffering. Many great and ruinous errors and faults are thereby cured or prevented. Miriam was taught to leave off her rebellious murmuring and trouble-making by being smitten with leprosy. Jonah was brought to his better senses and to the discharge of his prophetic duties by the trouble he encountered in the sea amid the storm of divine displeasure. David was recovered from his wandering from God by the afflictions that were sent upon him. Zacharias was cured of his unbelief by being struck with dumbness. Paul was kept from being exalted above measure by a humiliating and vexatious thorn in the flesh. And so afflictions of one sort or another are dealt out to the people of God for their spiritual profit, that the same may work out for them a far more exceeding and eternal weight of glory.

Up to the time the text was dictated the church at Laodicea appears to have been comparatively free from trouble. The members in general were outwardly prosperous and without the disturbances with which some of these churches had to contend. They counted themselves rich and happy and in need of nothing, and hence presumed that the special favor of Heaven was upon them. Their exemption from adversities made them think themselves particularly dear to the Saviour and spiritually blessed. But what they took as an argument that all was exceptionally well with them Jesus here retorts upon them as arguing the very opposite. Out of their own mouths He convicts them. Without rebuke and chastening they were wanting in one of the most essential proofs of His love. Excepted from these severe disciplinary dealings, they must needs be excepted from being sons. There was thus a very sharp and deep-reaching rebuke to their fond conceit when Jesus said to them, "*As many as I love I rebuke and chasten.*"

And yet if there were any poor, afflicted, or sorrowing ones among them, this announcement had much comfort in it for them. It said to such that as continued prosperity and sunshine in this world are no proof of the divine favor, but rather the contrary, so the presence of adversity and darkness do not prove the divine love withdrawn, but evidence its active presence.

When good Christian people are overtaken with misfortune and trouble, and fail of relief notwithstanding all their prayers and entreaties, they are apt to take it as a mark of God's anger and begin to wonder what great sin they have committed to deserve such punishment. But they mistake; it is not punishment at all. Instead of being retributive wrath, it is the manifestation of tender love. Trouble does not come because Jesus has ceased to love us, but because He does love us and is concerned to do the very best for us. The rule works both ways. As there is no love where there is no rebuke and chastening, so where the cross is there love is, graciously dealing with us for our greater good and blessedness.

But because these Laodiceans were happily free from adversity and trial, there was no reason in that for counting on the continuance of their boasted good-fortune. The very announcement to them of this principle in the Saviour's dealings was forewarning that they would either lose their salvation or would have to suffer like other saints. As prosperity had spoiled them, there had to come some sharp severity to correct them; and here was now the distinct pre-intimation that heavy judgment was at hand for them, to cure and save them if they properly received it, but destined to work great grief and their utter perdition if not allowed to set them right and induce in them a better temper. Nay, this judgment had now already set in. The very words that the Saviour was speaking were a part of it. In these they were now hearing from the throne in heaven the most distressing sentence upon them. By a tribunal from which there is no appeal their whole religious life and character is adjudged fatally defective, and so offensive that they would presently be ejected with disgust from all part or place with the Saviour if not promptly reformed and changed. From the very lips of Him in whom alone there was any hope for them they now were compelled to hear that all their supposed riches cloaked a wretched poverty, and that nothing could help them but instantaneous revolution in their thinking and their ways.

Here was judgment begun. Here were intense rebuke and chastening come, after all. Here were scourging and humiliation, severer even than the fires of the stake at Smyrna amid which Polycarp obtained the martyr's crown. What could cut deeper or burn into the soul a more torturing distress than such words from Christ Himself?

And yet it was not in anger, but in love, that these words were spoken. The intention was to recover, heal, and save, not to drive to despair. There was no hope for these people except in this way of dealing with them; and these very severities of reproof and menace were given in love, that those concerned might profit by them and set themselves to repair what was wanting.

What, then, was it that the Saviour wished to bring about in these people? There is never any activity of God in word or providence but it is meant to compass moral and practical results. In this case it was the rod of the word heavily applied, that the subjects of the affliction might be moved and incited to "*be zealous, **and repent.***"

Zeal means fire, warmth, boiling fervency—an earnest vehemence of all the affections in relation to God and His service. It is like wings to a bird, like wheels to a chariot, like sails to a ship, like the fire on which the engine depends for its steam and power; for it is the warmth and energy of soul by which a man throws himself into what he undertakes. Under the Law no sacrifice could be offered without fire; and no more can any service be rightly performed under the Gospel without zeal. There must be fervency and warmth, or all our devotions fail in power to rise acceptably to Heaven.

There may, indeed, be zeal without genuine service of God, against which to be on our guard.

There is a *hypocritical zeal*, like that of Jehu, who marched with fury and whose watchword was "The Lord of hosts," but who was more bent upon his own ambitious ends than on any service to be rendered to the Almighty. So also with the Pharisees, who paid tithe of mint, anise, and cummin, made broad their phylacteries, enlarged the borders of their garments, coveted the uppermost rooms at feasts and the chief seats in the synagogues, compassed sea and land to make proselytes, and for a pretence made long prayers, but did not hesitate to devour widows' houses, to set aside the weighty matters of judgment, mercy, and faith, to stone and kill the prophets, and to crucify the very Son of God.

There is also an *ignorant zeal*, like that of Saul of Tarsus before his conversion, or like that of the Jews, who had a zeal for God, but not according to knowledge. Such a zeal is like spirited mettle in a blind horse, hastening his speed only to break his neck.

There is likewise a *turbulent and bitter zeal*, driving one headlong beyond all bounds of propriety, place, moderation, and charity, like that of the unfledged apostles James and John, who thought to vindicate the honor of Christ by calling down fire from heaven to consume a whole village of Samaritans, or like that which, under color of religion or the maintenance of human rights, takes upon itself to massacre princes, overturn kingdoms, trample upon established law, break through all the bonds of society, and commit to the guillotine all who may stand in its way —a zeal kindled in hell rather than derived from heaven.

And yet there can be no genuine service of God without zeal. The ground-rule of the whole law of God and of all the precepts and requirements of His word is that if we are to serve God at all it must be with all the heart, with all the soul, with all the mind, and with all the strength. He is the Supreme, and if He is not the supreme in all our affections and activities we stand exposed to that consuming jealousy which will not allow of our having any other God besides Him.

Zeal in religion is not excitement, rant, and

fury. It is not fanaticism, bigotry, and intolerance. It is not a proud conceit of superiority which thanks God that it is not as other men, and draws its cloak of sanctity about it lest it should take on contamination by coming too near to them. It is not the heat of blustering passion, which must have the conflagration in which to live, and leaves only a burnt district when it retires. But it is the giving of the whole heart to Jesus and His service, so as not to draw back for any lure of this world or to stop at any sacrifice the Lord may require of us.

And just here was the particular deficiency of these Laodiceans. No charge of heresy in doctrine is made against them. No disorder in their services is alleged. Outwardly they were a prosperous and respectable community of Christians. But they were neither cold nor hot. They were lukewarm. *They had no zeal*, no fervency, no ardent warmth, no whole-souled earnestness in their Christianity. They were in an insipid and nauseating condition, which they needed to get out of, or nothing was to be hoped but to be spued out of the Saviour's mouth.

To get them out of this miserable lukewarmness it was now laid upon them to *repent*. Their mind had to be changed. Their whole estimate of things had to be revolutionized. Their good opinion of themselves had to be dropped. They were to go at the whole matter afresh, turn a new leaf, and begin again as poor sinners, destitute, blind, naked, and in peril of losing their salvation altogether. There was hope if they would now set out in good earnest, seek for a new baptism of the Spirit, and become alive and zealous in their profession and duties as Christians. But this was now an absolute requirement. If their wealth could not be consecrated to better uses than to inflate their self-consequence and self-complacency, it would prove their worst curse and be a chain about their necks to sink them to the deeper perdition. If they did not give themselves to more earnestness and heart-fidelity in their religion, their boasted outward prosperity would be to them their everlasting ruin. And nothing but a new start in a warm, devoted, and zealous spirituality, and a deepening of their piety in all directions, would now save them from an utter rejection by their Lord and Judge.

And if ever there was occasion for such demands, it is in the Christendom of our times. Never was the Church general and the great mass of its professed members so Laodicean in condition as in our days. Never was there so much joining of the worship of God with the worship of Mammon—such close affiliation of the Church with the world—so much boastful religiousness and churchism with so little genuine Christianity—so much self-confident profession with so much emptiness even in common honesty. People heap to themselves teachers to suit their tastes—teachers to slur over or deny unwelcome truths, flatter the vain imaginings of their hearers, and teach an easy-going way to heaven—and then think how wonderfully well off they are for this world and the next. Having come down to the world's ideas and gained the world's praise and patronage, they are full of the Laodicean self-sufficiency, and as full of Laodicean offensiveness to Christ.

Here and there we find some humble and devoted ones whom Jesus loves—some whom He bears upon His heart as His true saints. But they are mostly persons of whom the least account is taken—poor souls to whom nobody cares to listen or who are only despised as wishing to put a cowl upon the free spirit of this superlative age. The time prophesied of by Paul has come, when in the Church itself "men are lovers of their own selves, covetous, boasters, proud, blasphemers, heady, high-minded, lovers of pleasures more than lovers of God, having the form of godliness, but denying the power thereof." And it is useless for any of us to think that we are not more or less under the influence of this same Laodicean spirit; for that itself would be proof against us. What we all need is to repent and be zealous, that our religion may not be of that poor sort which Christ certainly will disown and reject.

It belongs to man to have live feelings. We cannot live without animation and passion. We must be interested and ardent in something. And if it is not in earnest spiritual Christianity and the service of God, it will be in the pursuits, follies, and caprices of this world, in the service of self and sin. The question is not whether we are to have warmth and zest in us, but whether the warmth and zest are to be for God and His Christ. *Feel* we must, and zealous we will be; but the question is whether our enthusiasm is to be nourished from the wells of salvation, or fed by the excitements and fascinations of the world, the flesh, and the devil.

The human family is not made up of lukewarm people. The whole world teems with activity and zealous effort. You look in vain for those who are not busy and earnest in something which lies near their hearts. Politics, science, literature, art, fashion, gain, promotion, riches, pleasure, sensuality,—all have their myriads of earnest devotees. Turn where we will, we find anxious faces, throbbing hearts, busy hands, agitated minds, and earnest souls. No one is lukewarm. Each has his subject to occupy and animate his thoughts and fire his zeal. The very weariness of the world proves the intensity of feeling which moves and tasks its heart. And if people are thus interested and earnest in the perishing things of this world, there can be no greater inconsistency, no worse unreason, no more offensive hypocrisy, than for them to claim to be Christians and yet have no zeal, no enthusiasm, no vigorous earnestness in what pertains to Christianity.

Everything else is in earnest. The world is in earnest. Christ is in earnest. The devil is in earnest, and all the devil's children are in earnest in one way or another. And for a professed Christian to hope to secure an eternal heaven without earnest and uncompromising endeavor to fill out the demands of his high calling is an anomaly in the universe, and a thing which the heavenly Judge can by no means tolerate. Hence His message to the Laodiceans, and to all in like condition: *"Be zealous, therefore, and repent."*

Dear friends, let us not deceive ourselves. If it is worth our while to be Christians at all, it is worth all the zeal, interest, and devotion we can give to it. If we have been lukewarm and indifferent, dividing our hearts between God and the things of the world, trying to keep up a name for discipleship while our feelings are left to run after the pleasures, gains, and honors of this life, the time has come for us to make a more serious matter of our religion. We must make an effectual end of all spiritual insipidity, or it will make an effectual end of our hopes. And unless we repent out of our lukewarmness, and make a more earnest showing that we really wish to have place among the Lord's redeemed, we may as well be assured, first as last, that we shall never get it; for only

> Shame and sorrow wait
> On feeble feet, faint heart, and wavering eyes.

Lecture Nineteenth.

Rev. 3: 20: "Behold, I stand at the door, and knock: If any man hear My voice, and open the door, I will come in to him, and will sup with him, and he with Me."

WHEN the Lord lifts His finger and says, *"Behold!"* we may be sure of something marked and marvellous to be considered. And so it is in this instance. God help us, therefore, to give heed!

Many have taken the text as the tenderest exhibit of the Saviour's condescending love contained in the Scriptures, but all the depths and implications of the passage are mostly unperceived. The picture is indeed very affecting and tender, but it does not refer so much to the Saviour's present attitude toward the unconverted as to His attitude toward the Church itself in the period of His second coming. Its particular reference is to that solemn time and that sad condition of things to which the Saviour alluded when He spoke the parable of the Unjust Judge and said, "Nevertheless, when the Son of man cometh, shall He find faith on the earth?" (Luke 18: 8). It contemplates Him as now in some sense absent, but as then arrived and in large measure barred out of His own Church.

The true application of the passage connects directly with a like presentation made in the Song of Solomon (chap. 5), some of the very language of which it repeats, and with the substance of which it coincides. In that marvellous Song the bride is always the Church and the Bridegroom the Lord Jesus. In that chapter the bride is represented in a sleepy and dreamy state in the midst of the night, neither dead asleep like the rest of the world, nor yet entirely awake, but in a state between the two, answering to the neither-hot-nor-cold condition of the Laodicean church. In this condition her Lord comes for her, and finds Himself locked out. He stands by the door and knocks and calls for admission, just as in the text. But so languid and slow is she to open to her Lord, and pleads so many dilatory excuses, that by the time she gets full awake, and would gladly receive Him, she finds to her sorrow that He has gone. Thus she is left to seek Him amid distresses, sufferings, and losses, just as the unready multitude will be "*left*" when the Lord cometh to take His watching and waiting people —"left" to experience the great tribulation, and amid its griefs to wash their robes that they may not be among the utterly lost.

In the same way the text identifies with what

the Saviour says in Luke (12 : 35–38), where He exhorts His people: "Let your loins be girded about, and your lights burning; and ye yourselves like unto men that wait for their lord, when he will return from the wedding; *that when he cometh and knocketh, they may open unto him immediately*. Blessed are those servants, whom the Lord when He cometh shall find watching: verily I say unto you, that He shall gird Himself, and make them to sit down to meat, and will come forth and serve them. And if He shall come in the second watch, or come in the third watch, and find them so, blessed are those servants." Here is precisely the same coming, the same knocking, and the same supping with those who open to Him, that we have in the text.

The presentation likewise coincides with what is recorded in Mark (chap. 13), where it is written, "The Son of man is as a man taking a far journey, who left his house, and gave authority to his servants, and to every man his work, and commanded the porter to watch. Watch ye, therefore; for ye know not when the master of the house cometh: at even, or at midnight, or at the cock-crowing, or in the morning. Lest coming suddenly, He find you sleeping. And what I say to you, I say unto all, Watch." The only difference is that the parable represents the coming to be in some indefinite time in the future, while in the text Christ is already come and standing before the door. Having been personally long absent, He at length returns to it in its last or Laodicean period, and knocks for admission. He comes to His own house, but His presence is not recognized nor His knocks responded to. The servants having lost all zeal, anxiety, and watchfulness for His return, and become indifferent and unbelieving in general, He finds them eating and drinking, revelling and fighting, according to the common course of the world, and saying one to another, No danger that the Lord will come in our day, if ever. And so the whole house is in disorder, the porter off his guard, and no one dreaming that it is Jesus giving His last merciful warning ere the great judgment breaks forth.

Accordingly, the showing here is that in the period of the Lord's second coming there will be a season in which He will be present with the signals that His long-promised return has come, but during which He will specially knock and plead and lift up His voice, that haply some may recognize His call, and welcome Him to their embrace and His rightful habitation. Though come with judgment-power to crush out everything that stands opposed to Him, He is loth to break in upon His wayward servants and consume them in His hot displeasure; therefore He stands and knocks, giving to His unready people one last warning and opportunity, and sending shrill and startling summons throughout Christendom that if any will share with Him the glorious marriage-supper they may open to Him, as otherwise they must meet the doom of those left to suffer with hypocrites and unbelievers in the great tribulation, from which all who are zealous in watching and prayer and accounted worthy to escape and to stand before the Son of man have been taken.

It was a sad and melancholy thing when, at the first advent, Jesus came unto His own and His own received Him not. But sadder still will it be when He comes again, having the complete fulfilment of all His promises in His hands, and the great body of His own Church does not know or acknowledge Him. It is bad enough when those who have never known Him, never counted themselves His friends, never tasted of His good word or the powers of the world to come, bar Him out from their affections and refuse to admit Him to their hearts; but for those baptized in His name, who have sworn allegiance to His authority, who profess to be marching under His flag, who have been entrusted with the guardianship of the treasures of His grace, word, and sacraments of love, not to know and acknowledge Him, to bar Him out of His own house, and to compel Him to stand outside knocking and begging that they may open to Him, is the superlative of human apostasy, ingratitude, and unfeeling depravity. Hence the exclamation, "Hear, O heaven, and give ear, O earth: I have nourished and brought up children, and they have rebelled against Me!"

And yet, as He prayed for His murderers at the time of His crucifixion, so He is loth to abandon and overwhelm His ingrate and degenerate Church, and at the last still holds His judgment back while He stands without and knocks, if haply some may open to Him, that He may come in to them and sup with them, and they with Him, and not fall under His consuming wrath.

There is indeed a sense in which the statement of the text is true during all the ages of the Church on earth. There is no time in which Jesus does not in a manner stand at the doors of those who hear His Gospel, knocking and calling for admission with His saving grace. In the course of nature He is in no one's heart, but outside. Yet He stands proposing Himself to each as the needed Saviour. By His word, Spirit, and providence He pleads and calls and knocks for admission. It is a great and precious truth, never to be lost sight of, that the very Lord of glory stands before every heart, applying for place and supremacy in it that He may be its Lord and Saviour. Thus He approaches every living soul among us, saying to it in many forms and intonations, "My son, give

Me thine heart." Often as He has been denied, He still continues to stand and call and wait and plead and knock. In every fresh message that sounds from the sacred desk, in every new stir of conscience, in every turn that awakens thought upon God, judgment, and eternity, His voice sounds, repeating again and again His gracious call, "*My son, give Me thine heart.*"

And when the voice of the word is disregarded He speaks and knocks with the voice of *the rod.* The schemes of life are hedged up and defeated, fond possessions are swept away, health is destroyed, life is brought into peril, death strikes into the home, trouble shakes the soul, and one stroke after another in loud detonation is made, to get the poor drowsy sleepers awake, to open unto Him and let Him in as their proper Lord and Saviour. And many a time and long has Jesus thus been standing and knocking at the hearts of multitudes who have persisted till now in disregarding His calls and proposals, and have become so habituated to their disregard of Him that some of these days they will have heard the last call of mercy, and neither hope nor help shall ever reach them more.

But the standing and knocking described in the text is something specific and peculiar. What Christ here says connects above all with the references in the other Letters, where He speaks of

His coming to remove the candlestick from those of His people who repent not of the evils into which they have fallen—His coming to fight against them with the sword of His mouth—His coming to relieve His suffering saints from all their burdens and to reward them that keep His works to the end—His coming as a thief to steal away His faithful watchers to Himself—His coming to keep those who keep the word of His patience out of that hour of dreadful trial which is then to come upon all the world—His second coming, when He cometh to reckon with His servants, having His reward with Him, to give to every man according as his work shall be,—that coming of which the Scriptures everywhere say so much, and of which the Church of our day really believes and understands so little.

The preaching of the Gospel and the ordinary operations of grace and providence in the conversion of sinners is never called *knocking* unless it be in this lone passage. Nor is knocking at a door to notify of one's presence suggestive of the ordinary calling of souls into the kingdom of heaven. Knocking gives the idea of a degree of violence which may be friendly indeed, but does not fall in with the common motions of grace. Preaching the Gospel is the proclamation of mercy in the name and stead of one absent, while knocking is the announcement of one present and newly arrived, and in a way very different from the beseeching of men to be reconciled to God. If it includes the ordinary operations of grace through the word, it unquestionably includes much more, and must be so understood. We find no such knocking spoken of in reference to either of the other churches. It has place only in the case of this church, with which the whole career of the Church in this world terminates by Christ's return to judge the quick and the dead. Nor is there any reference to Christ's second coming in all this Letter if not in this place. It must, therefore, in its more direct and particular meaning, belong to that period when the judgment is on the final verge of breaking forth upon the world—that period when Christ, if not already present unrevealed, is on the very point of ushering in the momentous scenes of the great consummation.

Precisely what this knocking is or is to be it is not given me to affirm, but it is unquestionably some loud enunciation of the personal presence of the Saviour returned to this world or of such an immediate nearness of Him in the great scenes of the judgment as to be the same as if here already. His coming as a thief would seem to imply that He will be present and at work unknown to the world, while many will only be convinced of the fact by the missing of what He has taken. And along with this coming as a thief in the night this knocking occurs. It would therefore seem to be some special indication of His presence, answering to a newly-arrived visitor's knock at the door to make known to the inmates that he has come—a knocking which those who are properly awake and waiting for Him will understand, and so respond as to be in position to welcome and receive Him to their everlasting blessedness.

The Scriptures everywhere tell us of many signs and portents to be given as that notable day draws near. Jesus Himself tells us, "There shall be signs in the sun, and in the moon, and in the stars; and upon earth distress of nations, with perplexity; the sea and the waves roaring; men's hearts failing them for fear, and for looking after those things which are coming on the earth: for the powers of heaven shall be shaken" (Luke 21 : 25, 26); and His word to His people is, "When these things begin to come to pass, then look up, and lift up your heads; for your redemption draweth nigh" (Luke 21 : 28). And the sending forth through all the regions of nature such agitations and alarms, with many other such disturbing manifestations prophesied of that time, would seem to answer best to this knocking of the Saviour as He stands before the door to give His last warning call to His drowsy Church.

And along with such signs and manifestations in the ordinary ongoing of things there will naturally and necessarily be the warning voice of many earnest servants of God, telling what these signs mean, and proclaiming aloud into the ears of a slumbering world that the hour of God's judgment is come, leaving no more time to be lost if they would have place in the ark of His salvation.

Three distinct commissions are given in the parable which sets forth the calling of guests to the Marriage of the King's Son. The first went forth to the Jews, so long notified beforehand, but who behaved so badly in the case that the King sent forth His armies and destroyed those murderers and burnt up their city. Then went forth a second commission to invite everybody from all the streets and lanes of the whole world. It is under this commission that the ministers of salvation have been acting from that time to this present. But the parable tells of a third and final commission. When the servants returned word that all was done as commanded, and yet there was room, the Lord said, "Go out into the highways and hedges, and *compel them* to come in, that my house may be filled." This last commission tells of a degree of force and violence in the fulfilment of it which differs from those preceding it, and shows the rising up of a class of preachers with unwonted point and constraining urgency in their messages, reinforced by the alarming condition of things all over, giving to the last appeals of mercy a degree of shrillness and compulsiveness never heard before. And this, it seems to me, is that particular note in the dispensations of God toward the drowsy Church and apostate world to which Jesus above all here refers. Standing as Judge before the door in the last extremity of time, He knocks by the signs and proclamations of His presence, that "if *any man*" hear His voice he may yet have part in the blessed marriage-supper of the Lamb.

And what, dear friends, if that time has already come and this knocking has already commenced? Far off it cannot be. The symptoms of its nearness are growing marvellously distinct, just as foretold, as all who will open their eyes may see. What a cry has of late years gone out over Christendom, and is now sounding from many pulpits, books, tracts, and platforms, in all lands and languages, saying, "*Behold, the Bridegroom cometh, go ye out to meet Him*"! Take the records of the last decade, or even the last five years, and when was there ever such uneasiness in the body of the earth, such disturbances in the seas, such singularities in the seasons, such marked violence in the motions of the elements, such unusual presentations in the conditions and relations of the heavenly orbs, such perplexing and ominous phenomena in the appearances of the sky? When was there ever such perturbed and ugly fermentation in the whole body of human society, such troubles, fears, distresses, embarrassments, and perplexities of nations, such discontent and rankling animosities between classes? When were there ever such numerous dark and bloody conclaves and combinations to set law at defiance, such disregard and overturning of the old landmarks and stabilities of the social fabric, such devilish passions plotting in secret and breaking out in all sorts of wicked disorder and destruction to life and property? When were there ever so many scandalous corruptions in public and private virtue, and such an unprecedented spread of unbelief, decay of faith, and popular infidelity, depleting our sanctuaries, infesting our schools and colleges, lurking in the hearts of half the professed Church, and cropping out even in the very pulpits? When was there ever such a multiplication and heaping up of fearful calamities and disasters of all sorts? Who cannot see for himself how outbreaking selfishness is everywhere pressing for supremacy, how lawlessness in lawmakers and in subjects is growing, how moral obligation is being trampled under foot by great and small, and how everything shakes and sways under the presence of a spirit which bodes only disaster and anarchy? And what does all this indicate but that the world to-day is verging upon the border-line of that dread time when God will let His judgment-thunders loose? Who can deny that the nations at this hour are treading over volcanoes that may any moment break forth and involve the world in ruins? And what, indeed, is to be made of all this, of which the newspapers are ever full—what can it mean—if it be not the great Judge standing before the door and knocking loud, that people may hear and answer in humble submission to His offers of mercy, lest they find themselves suddenly cut off for ever?

And if it should be that we are even a little beforehand in interpreting this to be the Saviour's final knocking in mercy to arouse us to a right reception of Him, we shall not lose by believing that it is, and ordering ourselves accordingly. It is very certain that these are the last days of grace for some of us, and it is quite possible that these may be the last days of grace and warning that the Church shall ever have; so that if we would at all cherish the hope of having place with Jesus at the great supper to which He has bidden us, the argument is as urgent and constraining as it can be made to stir us up to earnest repentance of all past negligence and sin and to arouse in us a zeal in all that is good and sacred, that by divine mercy we may not have our portion with the unprepared and unsanctified.

To this, then, dear friends, let us set ourselves with honest heart and firm trust, that when the Lord cometh we may be able to look up to Him and say, "Lo, this is our God; we have waited for Him, and He will save us: this is the Lord; we have waited for Him, we will be glad and rejoice in His salvation."

Behold, the Bridegroom cometh in the middle of the night,
And blest is he whose loins are girt, whose lamp is burning bright;
But woe to that dull servant whom the Master shall surprise
With lamp untrimmed, unburning, and with slumber in his eyes!

Lecture Twentieth.

Rev. 3 21: "To him that overcometh will I grant to sit with Me in My throne, even as I also overcame, and am set down with My Father in His throne."

THERE was a great promise contained in the verse last under consideration, which deserves more notice than then could be given it. Standing at the door and knocking, the promise of the Saviour is: "*If any man hear My voice and open the door, I will come in to him, and sup with him, and he with Me.*" Opening to Him is our work. He first comes to us. But then it is for us to answer to His signals and calls, to unlock the bolted doors, and to meet and greet Him as our blessed Lord and Redeemer. To enable us to do this His Spirit is always present to assist our natural weakness. And to any and every one who will thus open to Him He promises, first of all, *to come in*.

In the previous verses He presented Himself as a merchant from a far country, with refined gold and white raiment and healing medicines to bestow upon those willing to buy of Him or to come to terms with Him. Here the proposal is to become the familiar *guest* of those who open to Him the doors of their hearts and homes.

It may be very disturbing to have so great a Being come into onr unworthy dwellings. The thought of it may put us ill at ease. But Jesus is so good, so merciful, so benignly full of grace, that the moment He is admitted and begins to show His unspeakable tenderness and condescension the perturbation subsides and all dread disappears. Making Himself at home with us in our homes, sitting down with us at our tables, blessing our bread, entering into familiar communion with us as friend with friend, mercifully inquiring into our hardships and trials, gently speaking away the shame and burden of our unworthiness and sins, pouring upon us the rich treasures of His wisdom and grace, drawing us with the cords of a man into sweet converse about the blessed things to come, and warmly taking us into fellowship with His saving greatness, we are made to feel that we have reached the happiest day of our lives, and heaven itself seems to settle down upon our souls. And thus He offers to come in and *sup with us*.

But the further promise is to have us *sup with Him*. Entertaining Him, He proposes to entertain us. He means to give a supper to His saints —a supper proportioned to His greatness and goodness—at which He engages to give us place.

Receiving Him to sup with us at our earthly tables, He proposes to have us sup with Him at His heavenly banquet. And so great and glorious is the honor of place at that high festival that John was commanded to write, "*Blessed are they which are called unto the marriage-supper of the Lamb.*"

But in the verse now before us we have a still more exalted promise. We may call it the promise of promises; for it is the superlative of all the offers of grace. The Saviour here passes from gold and raiment and healing unction and social fellowship and festive communion to enthronement and everlasting regency.

When Christ was on earth He spoke of seats on His right hand and His left to be given to those for whom they are prepared. He also spoke of twelve thrones, on which His twelve apostles are to sit "when the Son of man shall sit on the throne of His glory." And so the apostles, by His inspiration, continued to preach and teach that "if we suffer with Him, we shall also reign with Him." In these and other places something of the royal prerogatives of His saints is implied. But nowhere in all the Scriptures do we find the immortal dignity of His faithful ones set forth in such distinct and impressive terms as in the text. More even than was promised to the apostles themselves is here promised to every true believer.

We are startled at the magnificence of the proposal: "*To him that overcometh will I grant to sit with Me in My throne, even as I also overcame, and am set down with My Father in His throne.*"

Two thrones are here brought into contemplation: the Father's throne, in which Jesus now is seated with the Father, and a second throne, which He calls *His own*, as distinguished from the throne of the Father.

When God brought His only-begotten into the world, and raised Him from among the dead, He not only commanded all the angels to worship Him, but said to Him, "Sit Thou on My right hand, until I make Thine enemies Thy footstool." Accordingly, we now "see Jesus, who was made a little lower than the angels for the suffering of death, crowned with glory and honor," "far above all principality, and power, and might, and dominion, and every name that is named, not only in this world, but also in that which is to come." And this is that throne of the Father on which Christ now sits as "Head over all things," "henceforth expecting till His enemies be made His footstool." It is not the throne of David, which remains to be established on Mount Zion, nor yet the throne of the Son of man, which all the kingdoms of the earth shall obey; but the absolute *God-throne*, invisible, yet omnipotent, not in the world, yet ruling over it, essentially spiritual because God is a Spirit, and for ever unchangeable and irresistible because eternal. It is the throne which only Godhead can occupy, and on which Christ sits coregent with the Father as the true and only Son of God. And this throne He will for ever share by reason of His Godhead. But as *the Christ*, He will not always remain upon the throne of the Father. We are told that there is a time coming when He will deliver it up and take another throne, of a more special and subordinate character, but more particularly *His* as the Son of man.

When on trial before Pontius Pilate, He professed to be a King, and declared that for this purpose He was born. Daniel says, "I saw in the night visions, and, behold, one like the Son of man came with the clouds of heaven, and came to the Ancient of days, and they brought Him near before Him; and there was given Him dominion, and glory, and a kingdom, that all people, nations, and languages should serve Him: His dominion is an everlasting dominion, which shall not pass away, and His kingdom that which shall not be destroyed." Hence, speaking of His second coming, Jesus says, "*Then* shall He (the Son of man) sit upon the throne of His glory, and before Him shall be gathered all nations." And so John in his vision of the coming forth of "the

Word of God" to destroy the Beast and false prophet, speaks of Him as crowned with many crowns and wearing on His vesture and on His thigh the invincible Name, KING OF KINGS AND LORD OF LORDS. And this is the *Christ-throne* as distinguished from the eternal *God-throne*. The one is the centre and summit of the absolute God-power; the other is the centre and summit of the subordinate Man-power, made sure and firm for ever in the God-man, the successful Redeemer.

Christ's throne, as distinguished from the Father's throne, is the throne of the Son of man— "that part of infinite power, that function and charge, which God originally intended man to occupy, and which Christ the Man-Redeemer of man shall occupy in the fulness of the times." It is not the throne of David merely, for that respects only the people of Israel; but it is *the throne of man* taken at its highest, as the Man Christ Jesus is the summation of all humanity. It is that throne which would have come to Adam had he never sinned, and which now cometh to Christ as the victorious second Adam, the Recoverer and Restorer of all things, and on which He is to reign for ever over the world He has redeemed. It is that throne of abiding dominion which comes into place when all the sovereignty of this world becomes the sovereignty of our Lord and of His Christ, and the Son of man takes the reins of empire over all the earth, in place of all the dragon-powers which now have the rule over it. And with reference to that throne the promise to every overcomer is that he shall share it with Christ, as Christ Himself also overcame and is set down with the Father on the Father's throne.

One of the marvels in this case is that this promise, for the first time so clearly given, is addressed to these faulty Laodiceans, whom Jesus had just now threatened to reject with loathing. But the more there is to be conquered, the greater the glory of the victory. The highest place is within reach of the lowest. The faintest spark of grace in the most unfavorable atmosphere may yet be fanned into the mightiest flame. Nor is there any one of us, or any sinner now walking on our streets, who may not rise by the vigor of penitence and faith in Christ to a place even with the King of glory on His everlasting throne.

Nor is it an empty honor or a meaningless ceremonial to be granted place with the Son of man on His throne. Not for parade-badges do the children of the resurrection get their dignities. Advanced to the throne of regency, they are not sham kings, any more than Christ's accession to dominion with the Father is a mere matter of form and ceremony. Titles and names are not

hollow designations in heaven. The session of
the Son of God on the right hand of eternal
Majesty is the putting of all power in His hands
and the putting of all things in subjection to Him,
leaving nothing but the eternal Father Himself
that is not put under Him. And like as Jesus is
set down with the Father on the Father's throne,
so every overcomer is to be set down with Jesus on
His throne. Whatever the offices of the throne
shall be, in the same shall all overcomers share.
Enthroned with Christ, they are to "reign with
Him," and participate in all the doings of His
kingdom and government. "Do ye not know
that the saints shall judge the world? . . . Know
ye not that we shall judge angels?" (1 Cor. 6:2,
3). Did not John in vision behold the saints
seated upon thrones, with powers of rulership
put into their hands, and living and reigning
with Christ in holy and immortal dominion?
Does not the Psalmist celebrate it as the final
honor of all the saints, "to execute vengeance
upon the heathen and punishments upon the
people; to bind their kings with chains, and
their nobles with fetters of iron; to execute upon
them the judgments written"? (Ps. 149:6–9).
Hath not the Saviour Himself said, "Verily,
verily, I say unto you, He that believeth on Me,
the works that I do shall he do also, and greater
works than these shall he do"? (John 14:12).

As kings with Christ the saints are to fill the place and do the work of kings. They are to "*reign with Him*" as truly as ever Solomon or David reigned, and as truly as the Son of man Himself shall reign.

The end of our salvation is not to sit on clouds and sing psalms, or to luxuriate in the idle bliss of an eternal languor and ecstasy. The life of Christ upon His Father's throne is an intense and busy life, administering the kingdom of the universe; and the life of the saints consociate with Him on His throne is to be in its degree of the same sort. They are called, redeemed, and glorified for sublime regency with their Lord; and in whatever pertains to the administration of His kingdom as the Son of man they are to participate, being joined with Him then as the angels are joined with Him now in the administrations of the God-throne; yea, and in still closer union, for by His saving grace they are related to Him on the human side as He is related to the Father on the divine side.

But such exalted dignity and honor do not come without earnest effort and hard conflict. Only the *overcomers* are to sit with Christ on His throne. There are battles to be fought and risks to be run and enemies to be vanquished and difficulties to be conquered before we are eligible or prepared for such transcendent promotion.

One of the most common images under which the Scriptures set forth Christian life is that of a fight—a heavy conflict with powerful hindrances and enemies. It is constantly reiterated in these Letters. Every true Christian is a soldier and has a warfare on hand to fight through to victory. This is the picture everywhere.

The particular trouble with these Laodiceans was their lukewarmness, their worldliness, their boastful self-complacency, their lack of deep and earnest spirituality. With this, therefore, their particular fight was to be. Their easy-going in the matters of faith and devotion was to be vanquished and a better order of things maintained. And on this field they were required to overcome before they could inherit this glorious promise.

But their case was not peculiar. In all ages and places this same trouble is to be met. It is the particular trouble with the Church of our day. The half-Christian and half-worldly condition of modern religionists is destroying the souls of many who think themselves well on the way to heaven. This, then, is the enemy which we must fight and conquer if we would reign.

But various and many are the Christian's foes. Deep within us and everywhere around us they rise up to keep us from the prize. In our own hearts great hosts of them are lodged. Here are thousands of promptings to unbelief and self-indulgence, multitudes of lusts after evil things, and many uprisings of bad temper, pride, ugly passions, and evil dispositions.

Along with these inward enemies are many outward ones to reinforce them. Our lives lie through a world adverse to God and holiness—a world full of gayeties and follies, cares and vexations, false maxims and unholy ways, flattering promises and treacherous caresses, and a thousand things to hinder a life of faith and godliness.

And back of all is the great combination of evil spiritual powers, the devil and his angels, ruling in the children of disobedience and ever active in using their hold upon the world and human nature to prevent the rise and progress of faith and righteousness. Our wrestling is not with flesh and blood only, but with principalities and powers, those that rule in the darkness of this world and infest the whole realm of the air we breathe.

These spiritual enemies are insidious, and have many ways of access to our hearts and feelings, to catch away or stifle the good and to incite to evil. Though under limitations and constraints, we need to be on special guard against their wiles and cunning assaults, and nothing but vigorous resistance can protect us from their snares and wicked machinations.

It is hence impossible for any one to be carried to heaven on a flowery bed of ease. Every inch of the way is disputed by adverse influences and subtle foes. And if we are to get through in ultimate triumph we must fight and keep up the conflict unto victory.

Considering the number and power of these enemies, and the poverty of our strength, we might well despair. But Christ has conquered for us, and has made it possible now for every one of us to conquer also through His strength and grace. Evil is not omnipotent: It is under ban, and the promise of the Almighty is that if we are true to ourselves and to Him, He will not suffer us to be tempted beyond what we are able to bear. He hath appointed for us the weapons of success, and put them at our command for every emergency, whether for defence or attack. With God's truth we may amply gird our loins. The righteousness of Jesus serves as an effectual breastplate. There is Gospel provision to protect our feet. Faith is a shield wherewith to quench the fiery darts of the wicked one. An already-wrought salvation is an ample helmet. The word of God is the sword of the Spirit by which to hew our way through all opposing ranks. Prayer ever keeps open communication with the heavenly throne for all needful supplies. And from Him who sits upon it the assurance is: "My grace shall be sufficient for thee." There is now, therefore, no doubt of our success if only we set ourselves to conquer and use the means provided for our victory. But there must be honest effort and determined perseverance to bring us through.

We know how Jesus overcame. We know the devotion with which He gave Himself from the beginning to be about His Father's business. We know how meekly He came to receive baptism from John in His earnestness to fulfil all righteousness. We know with what steadfastness He endured and foiled the temptations of the devil against all the solicitations of carnal appetite, worldly ambition, and challenges to prove Himself the Son of God. We know with what earnestness and fidelity He pursued His sacred mission, and in all His trials committed Himself unto God as unto a faithful Creator. We know with what zeal He kept up His constant prayers and communings with Heaven amid the exhausting toils of earth. We know with what holy meekness He submitted to abuse, torture, shame, and death that He might fulfil the purpose of the Father in sending Him into the world. And we also know the result—how that He thus overcame and is set down with the Father upon the throne of eternal Majesty, "leaving us an example that we should follow His steps," and thus overcome as He overcame, and sit with Him on His throne as He overcame and is set down with His Father on the Father's throne.

Dear friends, it may cost us heavily in these last evil times to maintain ourselves in true and faithful Christian life; but the glory to be gained is worthy of it. Hot and trying as the battle with self and sin may be, the victory is sure and the reward is a place with Jesus on His everlasting throne. Therefore, let us not be weary of the strife nor ever give up the fight. Heaven is with us in our efforts. Victory must come if we flinch not, and immortal regency is the goal of our honest fidelity.

Some, indeed, have thought it an ill covetousness of honor for us poor mortals to aim and strive for such high place in the world to come. They speak of it as savoring of carnal desire to think of attaining crowns and reigning as kings. And some appear to regard it as a token of their superior modesty that they never indulge in such lofty ambition and have no wishes for princely dominion. But such people do greatly mistake what true spirituality is. We are exhorted to "covet earnestly the best gifts." Jesus Himself again and again speaks of crowns, and holds them forth to our view as the prize of our high calling, and charges each Christian to be diligent and hold fast that no one take his crown. And here the direct promise is, that whosoever shall press the good fight of faith through to victory He will grant to sit with Him in His throne, as He overcame and is set down upon the Father's throne. And shall we take it for piety to charge Him with extravagance and falsehood in the promises He gives to His people? Shall we put the lie upon what issues from our Saviour's lips, and call it devout modesty?

I cannot but regard it as a sorry humility which claims to be more spiritual than Jesus and to know better than He what is fitting to be set before us as the goal of our Christian devotion. Is it not a pitiable meekness which would say to the glorious Son of God that we have no wish for His offered thrones, and that to sit and reign with Him is something we do not desire? Is it not a poor appreciation of what He has secured for us, and bordering on unfaith itself, to decline aspiration to what is held forth to us as the prize for which we are to aim? Alas, alas, for the miserable lassitude of spirit, the gross indifference, the hazardous questioning of the divine promises, and the dangerous doubting of the Saviour Himself, for us to put away from us all thought and effort to share these exalted honors! And if we do not care to have them, we may be sure we shall never get them, and the danger is that we may never reach heaven at all. To despise dominion or to speak evil of dignities certainly is not one of the things belonging to proper saintship.

Let us beware, then, how we undervalue the

proposals and promises of our Saviour. Let us rather rejoice and be glad that He hath made it possible for us to become immortal princes, to reign with Him on His throne, and to share the dominion of the world to come. And as we value eternal kinghood let us bestir ourselves all the more earnestly to "fight the good fight of faith," knowing that there is laid up for us a crown of righteousness, which the Lord the righteous Judge shall give us at that day, and not to us only, but to all them that love His appearing.

> Thou Crucified! the cross I carry,
>   The longer may it dearer be;
> And, lest I faint while here I tarry,
>   Implant Thou such a heart in me
> That faith, hope, love may flourish there,
> Till for my cross THE CROWN I wear!

Lecture Twenty=first.

Rev. 3 : 22: "He that hath an ear, let him hear what the Spirit saith unto the churches."

THESE words bring us to the conclusion of these sacred Letters of our Lord. For the seventh time in the course of these addresses they are here repeated. But they do not appear in the same place in each instance. In the first three Letters they precede the final promise, and in the last four they follow that promise. The change seems to be connected with the growth of evil in the Church. In the first and purer churches these words are spoken more from within, and in the case of those in which the evil preponderated they are spoken more from the outside.

There is such a thing as grieving the Holy Spirit, and thus diminishing His gracious influences. We read of a place in which Christ did not many mighty works because of the unbelief of the people. So, as the Church lapses from truth, purity, and love, and takes up with what is contrary to Christ, He is in some sense forced away from it, and His communications come to it more from without and from a distance than from the intimacies of a close fellowship and nearness. The apostle tells us that drawing nigh to God, He draws nigh to us; and the converse of this must also be true. And as the last four of these churches show more evil in them than good, the Saviour ceases to speak this word as from within the Church, and speaks it from the outside—not, indeed, as having abandoned His Church, but as having been in measure pushed out of that thorough oneness with it which existed in better times.

But whether this is the true reason for this studied change of the position of this call or not, the words themselves have great significance, which we should not fail to lay to heart.

I. We are here assured that the Lord hath spoken and given to men a revelation of His mind and will. At sundry times and in divers manners God spake in time past unto the fathers by the prophets; and in these last days He hath spoken by His Son, whose words have been confirmed unto us by them that heard Him. And in these seven Letters we have a special word from heaven. He who dictated them is the Alpha and Omega, the First and the Last, He who hath the seven spirits of God and holdeth the keys of death and hell, the Son of God, the Amen, the Beginning of the creation of God. What He utters He also authenticates as "what the Spirit saith." John also records the same as "words of prophecy," received when "in the spirit," and given him from the invisible heavenly world to be made known to the churches. There is then a word of God on earth to teach us the true mind and will of Heaven.

II. We are here assured that these divine utterances are intended for all people. The call of the text is as universal as language can make it. Every one that hath an ear is called upon and admonished to "hear what the Spirit saith unto the churches." The meaning is not merely that every one in Ephesus was to give attention to what was written to the angel of the church in Ephesus, that every one in Smyrna should hear what was written to the angel of the church in Smyrna, and so on of the several communities in these several cities. Nor is the meaning simply that all in these several cities were to be careful to consider all these several Letters. There were then, and have been since, and are now, very many other people having ears to hear. You and I and all men the world over have ears to hear, and are as well capacitated by nature and grace to take in these messages as the people who then lived. And wherever there is an ear to hear, to that ear is addressed "what the Spirit saith unto the churches."

These Letters of Jesus are thus divinely put forward for *our* instruction and profit equally with any who lived before our time. Each of these several churches was of course expected to give special heed to what was specially addressed to it; and so also each Letter had its special application, prophetic and otherwise, to its particular period in the successive ages of the Church's earthly career; but all was for all in every age, and for us now as well as for any other people.

I cannot therefore but think that the Church in these later times has done injustice to herself and behaved unseemly toward her Lord in not assigning these Letters of Jesus a higher and more distinguished place in the Lessons set to be read in her worshipping assemblies. There is no richer portion of Scripture; there is no portion made up more exclusively of the words of Christ; nor is there another portion so solemnly, so urgently, or with such special sanctions pressed upon the attention of all who would be Christians. And yet in proportion to the imperativeness of the Saviour's call to hear what He has thus given has been the dereliction of the Church of the last thousand years to neglect it. This should not so be. And as men would honor Jesus, and be true to His word as our Lord and Judge, I call upon them to repent and reform from this ill way of dealing with these momentous messages from His throne. They are His messages to His professing Church of all time. And I cannot see how people are to fulfil their duty as Christ's disciples, and yet ignore and neglect these His last and most special communications as if they were of no particular interest to us. Dear friends, let us not share in that neglect.

III. We are here assured that the contents of these Letters are of transcendent import. Our Saviour repeatedly used exactly similar expressions when He was on earth, and always in connection with things of vital character. It was a vital thing for the Jews to understand the character, mission, and testimony of John the Baptist. It is a thing of vital moment to understand the operations of grace and our duty with regard to the same. Momentous are the facts touching the nature and condition of the kingdom of heaven in this world, the ending up of things at the termination of the present dispensation, and the ultimate fate of the tares and the wheat. It is of very great account for us to know what is spiritual defilement and spiritual purity, and what is true and consistent righteousness before God. And for the people who live in the last perilous days of the great Antichrist nothing is more important than to be able to identify the Beast and to know the speedy and inevitable perdition of all who worship him and receive upon them his mark. But it is with reference to these very things, and these only, that these particular words are used. In each of those instances they are given but once, while here they are uttered seven times, and each time including the whole body of these Letters. Unquestionably, then, in the mind and estimate of the Lord we have here what is of superlative doctrinal and practical importance. If the same truths may be fragmentarily gathered from other parts of Holy Scripture, we have them here in concrete and formal summation and practical application, such as we find not elsewhere.

If we would know the true nature, offices, and glory of our divine Lord and Redeemer, we here have Him presented and described by Himself in sententious fulness and originality beyond any other part of the sacred word.

If we would know the nature, organization, relations, dangers, duties, and career of the Church, how its responsibilities are distributed, and what in any department or period of its history is approved or disapproved by Christ, and how in any case it must fare in His judgment, we have it here most succinctly given in His own words.

If we would know wherein true Christian life

or saintship consists, with what sort of dangers and conflicts it is beset in this world, in what temper and attitude we are to keep ourselves with regard to our various relations and surroundings that we may come off conquerors at the last, there is no place where the same is more vividly set forth.

If we would know exactly what Jesus thinks of the many grave matters which have developed among Christian professors in the several ages of the Church, and which still agitate, divide, and distract it, we here have His mind upon them direct from His throne. Every honest and faithful student can here see how He puts His finger upon each particular, and speaks His words of praise or of condemnation. We may find elsewhere what, if rightly applied, would conduct us to the same conclusions; but we have here not only principles whose applications we must infer and reason out in our weak and uncertain way, but the facts and conditions themselves are brought under the all-penetrating eye of the Saviour and authoritatively pronounced upon by Him. Indeed, we here have the mind of Christ with reference to all important developments, tendencies, systems, and conditions in the Church from the beginning till now, in a form much less mistakable and more direct than anywhere else.

And if we would know what is to be the future

of the saints after this present order of things comes to an end, and get a deep insight into the life and honors which the second coming of Christ is to bring to His redeemed ones, the several promises in these Letters present a body of particulars in this regard unexcelled by any other part of Scripture. A completer description of those good things which Jesus has in reserve for His true and faithful people is not found in all God's word. All commonplace ideas of heaven are here put to utter shame as not reaching so much as the first syllables of the sublime charter of the rights and honors forepledged to us by our Lord.

These are things of priceless value, and fully warrant all the urgency with which they are pressed upon universal attention.

IV. We are here assured that it is the will of our Lord that we should earnestly study and practically apply what is given us in these Letters, and dispose our thinking, hopes, and activities accordingly. Nothing less than this is included in the *hearing* to which the text refers. To hear only with the outward ear, to have a mere intellectual acquaintance with what has thus been dictated from heaven, does not fulfil the audience the Saviour calls for. Having given us ears, He has given His word that we may use our ears to take it in, and thus to ponder it and profit by it. The admonition corresponds to what was said at the opening of the book, where it is written, "Blessed is he that readeth, and they that hear the words of this prophecy, *and keep those things which are written therein.*" It is the same that the Saviour elsewhere relates of the good-ground hearers, "who in an honest and good heart, having heard the word, keep it, and bring forth fruit with patience."

There is a hearing which so lacks in appreciation or is accompanied with such indifference that the devil has no trouble in preventing it from making any practical impression on the heart. There is also a hearing which for a while entertains and believes, but is content with such a superficial regard, and takes in only to such shallow depths that all good from it soon wilts and perishes. There is also a hearing with every promise of thrifty growth and ample harvest, which, however, allows itself to be so invaded "with cares, riches, and pleasures of this life" that they choke and smother proper fruitfulness. But all such hearing falls far short of the hearing demanded in the text. This is a hearing which gives earnest and studious attention, which takes the matter to heart in all the depths of the soul, and which allows nothing to interfere with a devout, practical, and persevering conformity to what is heard and learned.

These pictures of Jesus, His glory, power, offices, all-searching knowledge, and infallible judgments, are spoken directly to the heart, that they may affect and move us to right faith and fear. These sharp rebukes and sentences upon wrong are for us to take home to our souls, that we may get us out of everything thus condemned and stand in awe of the solemn threatenings of our Lord. These gracious encouragements and grand promises are meant to take hold of our imaginations, quicken our heavenly desires, and inflame our anticipations, that the vain things of this world may dwindle from our regard and our whole affection be set on the things above. Nor have we rightly heard "what the Spirit saith unto the churches" till we come to this temper and state of mind and heart; for the Gospel is not to be to us a thing of word only, but of power.

V. And yet one other important matter is signified in the text; and that is the intensely personal character of what is here demanded. The Saviour is addressing ministers and congregations, but after all it is the separate individuals that are to give ear and do this hearing.

We are apt to lose ourselves in the mass. The community, the country, the church, the general body, is prone to preoccupy the attention, while we lose sight of the individuals of which every society is made up. But it is the nature of Christianity to single out and give importance to the individual man and woman. It deals not with people in masses, but with each soul separately, and by working upon and from the individual it seeks to affect and condition society. As the builder takes stone by stone to build his walls, so Christ takes people one by one to make up His Church; and there is neither sanctification nor Church except as individual souls are moved and sanctified and personally brought into right relations to God.

Hearing is a personal thing. It cannot exist apart from the individual who hears. Others cannot hear for us if we do not hear for ourselves. The Church, the community, the society cannot hear for us if there is no hearing on the part of the individuals who compose them. One man cannot believe for another man, any more than we can eat or sleep for one another. Each must do his own repenting, believing, and serving of God, just as he must die for himself and stand in the judgment for himself. And hence the hearing of which the text speaks is devolved upon each individual soul the same as if no others existed.

It is very significant that while the church, the congregation as a whole, is rebuked, reprimanded, encouraged, exhorted, or advised, the promise is always to the *individual* and in the singular: "To *him* that overcometh;" "*He* that overcometh;" "Be *thou* faithful unto death, and I will give *thee* a crown of life." And so the command in each instance is: "*He* that hath an ear, let *him* hear what the Spirit saith unto the churches." What is said to the body it is made the duty of each individual person to deal with for himself and herself. We cannot go to heaven under our neighbor's cloak. We cannot shift our individual responsibilities to other people's shoulders. We cannot hide ourselves in the multitude when we come before the bar of God. Not as others view Christ, but as we individually view Him—not as others hear His voice, love, honor, and obey Him, but as we for ourselves do it—not as others believe and strive and overcome, but as we personally take hold and press our own way to victory—are we to inherit the promises. And until we learn to file out singly in these matters of grace and salvation, and individually hear, appropriate, and act, no paradise, no crown, shall we ever reach.

Dear friends, how is it, then, with us? To what extent have these sacred Letters of our Lord served us "for doctrine, for reproof, for correction, for instruction in righteousness"? We have been lingering long over these solemn communications of Jesus to His churches. Have we been giving to them a reverent ear and an attentive heart? Very many precious truths, like pearls from heaven, have met us in the way. Have we seized upon them as they came and appropriated them for the enrichment of our souls? Many sweet sounds of heavenly music have fallen upon us from the lips of our glorified Saviour. Have they served to charm away our hearts from the strifes and scrambles of earthly greed and the solicitations of earthly vanities? We have been hearing of many stern rebukes for decline in first love, for departures from the pure faith, for hypocritical zeal and false profession, for worldly conformity and the indulgence of worldly lusts, for the wearing of a name to live while dead in trespasses and sins, for the self-complacent and self-deceived who think they are rich and increased with goods and have need of nothing, while wretched and miserable and poor and blind and naked. Have we then taken them to heart, and tried ourselves by the demands of God, and set ourselves to honest repentance where we have found ourselves included among the faulty? We have been hearing many blessed commendations of labors and sufferings and patience and unflinching perseverance in duty for the sake of Christ's name, and of the sublime rewards held out to every overcomer who is faithful unto death. Have they had the effect to inflame our zeal, to strengthen our resolves, to encourage our hearts, and to wed us to the word of Christ's patience? Certainly we have been brought very close to divine things. The light of heaven has been streaming over and about us. The Lord Jesus in His glory, in His survey of those who profess to be His people, in His threatenings to the defective, and in His solemn judgments, has come very near to us. And great responsibilities are thus devolved upon our souls. Have we, then, been made better and furthered in our spirituality by what we have been called to contemplate? We have been compelled to look at the approaching outcome of the whole present order of things, at the certain nearness of the end, at the coming tribulation which is to overtake this wicked world and all who have not made clean their escape from its sins and vanities, and how only those who watch and pray always and keep the word of Christ's patience shall be kept out of the dreadful calamities which then shall come. Has it, then, moved us to the girding up of our loins, the trimming of our lamps, and the setting of ourselves in the attitude of men that wait for their Lord, that when He cometh and knocketh we may open unto Him immediately?

Dear friends, my heart is full, it is enlarged with desire, it swells with anxiety, that all who hear me on these great themes may be rightly advised of the truth and made alive to all that is contained in these messages of the Spirit. Here is light. Here is blessedness. Here is salvation. Here is glory everlasting. Here is the tree of life. Here is the crown of life. Here are the hidden manna and the white stone with the new name. Here are power and dominion and the possession of the Morning Star. Here are the white raiment of saintly dignity, enrolment with the celestial citizens, and acknowledgment by the King before the eternal Father and His angels. Here are inbuilding and incorporation with the heavenly temple as pillars of beauty and glory, inscribed with the name of God and the name of the city of God and the new name of the great Redeemer. Yea, here is place at the marriage-supper of the Lamb, and place with Jesus on His throne as He has place upon the Father's throne. And all is put within our reach and reserved for every one who will "fight the good fight of faith, laying hold on eternal life." Let us appreciate and improve our privileges. Prophets and kings desired to see the things we see, and have not seen them, and to hear the things we hear, and have not heard them. Such opportunities can come to us but once, and the time of them is here and rapidly passing away. Any day the summons of God's trump may come to His believing and ready ones, saying, "Come up hither." And so, then, if any one hath an ear, let him hear what the Spirit saith unto the churches.

Jesus is ready to hear us. He bids *us* ask of Him whatsoever we need, and promises that we shall not ask in vain. Shall we not, then, give earnest heed to all His word, and ever pray that it may be to us the bread of life?

> Far, far away, like bells at evening pealing,
>   The voice of Jesus sounds o'er land and sea,
> And laden souls, by thousands meekly stealing,
>   Kind Shepherd! turn their weary steps to Thee.
>
> Rest comes at length; though life be long and dreary,
>   The day must dawn and darksome night be past;
> All journeys end in welcomes to the weary,
>   And heaven, the heart's true home, will come at last.

www.ingramcontent.com/pod-product-compliance
Lightning Source LLC
Chambersburg PA
CBHW050430240426
43661CB00055B/2328